Kent

40 favourite walks

published by
pocket mountains ltd
The Old Church, Annanside,
Moffat DG10 9HB

ISBN: 978-1-907025-983

Text and photography copyright © Ben Giles 2023

The right of Ben Giles to be identified as the Author of this work has been asserted by him in accordance with the Copyright, Designs and Patents Act 1988

A catalogue record for this book is available from the British Library

Contains Ordnance Survey data © Crown copyright and database 2023 supported by out of copyright mapping 1945-1961

Printed by J Thomson Colour Printers, Glasgow

MIX
Paper | Supporting
responsible forestry
FSC® C023105

Introduction

For many people, their first experience of Kent may well be one of racing through the county at many times the average walking pace. Holidaymakers rushing by road for the crossing to the continent from Dover and Folkestone have been speeding along Kent's two major motorways and dual carriageways for more than half a century now.

For those entering the county at the Dartford Crossing over the River Thames or quitting London through Beckenham, Bromley and Sidcup, their first view of the Kent countryside often comes where the M20 funnels its traffic up through the long cutting over the North Downs and swiftly down towards Maidstone or on the M2 and A2 between the downs and the coast, sweeping without pause past Rochester, Chatham, Sittingbourne, Faversham and Canterbury, with the briefest of glimpses over the flatlands of the Hoo Peninsula and the Isle of Sheppey to the glimmerings of the Thames Estuary beyond.

For those orbiting south of London through Surrey on the M25, Clacket Lane Services signal the approach of the county border, where Biggin Hill and the escarpment of the North Downs above Chevening beckon on the left, while to the right there stretches out the enticing northern edge of the High Weald beyond Westerham and Sevenoaks. Nearing Maidstone, the North Downs briefly recede as the River Medway invites you to join its meandering way through to the coast before the chalk once more rises on the left. Now motorway and high-speed railway duel for space as they criss-cross each other at the foot of the downs past signs for Lenham and Charing to Ashford. In a final swing left to avoid Romney Marsh, the chalk hills crowd in again by Sellindge and Folkestone where the Channel Tunnel delves under the sea, and on over the white cliffs and down into Dover the ferries ply their way across the sea-lanes to France.

Yet as those who have ever turned off the motorways or lived in the county's towns and villages well know, Kent has much more to offer than just a high-speed link to the continent. Within the distance covered by a long summer's day walk or half a day's bike ride, you can pass from capital city to coastal port, from tidal saltmarsh to high chalk downs, from riverside meadows to Wealden woodland. North of the main central travel corridor lies the North Kent coast and the tidal estuaries of the River Medway and The Swale. The towns and settlements of this part of the county have a long and important history, if diminished now from their heyday as ports and commercial centres, though there is plenty of industry still surviving. The area around the North Downs in the centre of the county, despite being enclosed by two parallel motorways, continues to maintain and preserve its local distinctiveness and is as good walking country as any other stretch of chalk downs in southern England. To the south lies the mixed farming countryside of the Weald where, perhaps more than anywhere else in the county, the pressure of commuter-belt housing and the expansion of towns is most visible. Yet the Weald still offers some of the most picturesque walking routes to be found in the South East of England. Off the main travel routes in the northeast past Canterbury are the floodplains of the River Stour, beyond which the Isle of Thanet, until medieval times separated by the wide Wantsum Channel, gives access to the coastal cliffs and bays around North Foreland and the towns of Whitstable, Herne Bay, Margate and Broadstairs. Stretching southeastwards from the former Cinque Port of Hythe to the county border with Sussex lies the open expanse of Romney Marsh and its fringe of sandy beaches on the sweep of coastline around to the shingle headland of Dungeness. All of this makes Kent one of the most varied counties in England for exploring on foot.

About this guide

This guide contains 40 routes ranging in length from an hour's stroll to half a day's walking, divided into five sections broadly based on the topography of the county. Most of the routes are intended as comfortable walks or strolls. On some

routes the cumulative ascent or some steeper escarpments of the downs may require greater exertion than the strict route length suggests, but in general the walking is on well-worn paths, lanes and tracks, with plenty of waymarks, which should require minimal time and effort for route-finding. The route descriptions concentrate on the salient points of navigation, but may not cover every twist or turn. If in doubt, the obvious path is usually the line to take. In addition, the accompanying sketch maps serve an illustrative purpose and, for the longer or more complex routes, it would be a good idea to have access to the relevant OS Explorer mapping, details of which are given at the start of each walk.

The recommended time for each walk is an estimate based on an average walking speed of 4kmph, with a small allowance added in on some hillier or clifftop routes. However, timings will vary significantly, not only for individuals but also given the seasonal effects on paths, especially those crossing fields, or tracks on the downs, sections of which can become muddier and more slippery at certain times of year. A few routes also pass along cliff edges, tidal estuaries or coastline subject to tides, which can become unavailable depending on the state of the tide. Most paths covered in the routes are well-used and well-maintained by local agencies, but, in spring and summer especially, hedges and undergrowth grow vigorously and nettles, brambles and thorn can infiltrate narrower paths, stile crossings and gates. It is hoped that there is plenty of interest along the routes themselves and it would be possible to spread a short walk over half a day if time is taken to explore along the way. Conversely, some of the routes are short enough to attempt two in a day.

Getting around and access

Many of the main towns in Kent can serve as useful bases for walking. In the west of the county, Sevenoaks and Tunbridge Wells lie closest to London and neighbouring Surrey. Along the north coast are Rochester, Sittingbourne and Faversham, which give easy access to the Hoo Peninsula and the Isle of Sheppey. The county town of Maidstone and nearby Ashford are well-placed for exploring some of the Low and High Weald, while the small towns of Hythe and Tenterden are convenient for southeastern parts. Finally, the ancient cathedral city of Canterbury provides an historic setting for exploring the east of the county, while the towns of Margate, Deal, Dover and Folkestone have long been popular coastal resorts.

Almost all these towns have railway stations and regular bus routes branching out from them. An effort has been made to start walks from places which are served by public transport and it would usually be possible to plan the completion of a walk from a town to coincide with train times. It is worth noting that it is increasingly the case that many of the villages in Kent are only intermittently served by public bus on both a weekly or seasonal basis. Access by car is still the preferred option for many and, while towns cater adequately for parking, this can be a sensitive issue in smaller villages and hamlets. Pubs and inns can be very accommodating if the intention is to visit before or after a walk, but where parking is outside designated car parks, consideration should be shown for the needs and access of local residents and the farming community.

Kent is still substantially a rural county and has traditionally been associated with mixed farming, including fruit and hops, and, in some areas, sheep, arable and dairy farming can all be encountered in the space of a single walk. At lambing time, signs on gates may well request that dogs are kept on a lead and the presence of dogs for cows can be problematic – it is not unheard of for cows with calves to behave in a very protective way. Even without a dog, cattle just released from winter shelters or cows which have recently calved should be left well alone. If in doubt, it is usually advisable and possible to find a short detour to avoid such livestock.

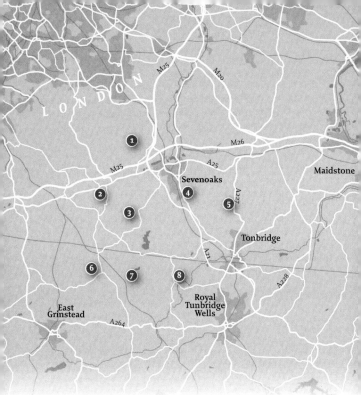

In the west of the county is to be found an area very similar to the eastern edge of the Surrey Hills, located just across the county border, and dominated by the two large towns of Sevenoaks and Tunbridge Wells. North of the M25 the chalk slopes of the North Downs mark the limits of Greater London, while to its south the Greensand Ridge stretches eastwards over Crockham Hill and Ide Hill above the small town of Westerham towards Sevenoaks. To the east and south of Sevenoaks are a number of historic houses and parks, Knole and Ightham Mote being two of the best known. Further south lies the Eden Valley, beyond which the rolling countryside on the northern edge of the High Weald around the villages of Chiddingstone and Penshurst leads to Tunbridge Wells, not far from the border with Sussex.

The view east from St Mary's Church, Westerham ▶

Sevenoaks and Tunbridge Wells

Knockholt Pound and Chevening Park

Distance **6km** Time **1 hour 45**
Terrain **lanes, fields and parkland**
Map **OS Explorer 147** Access **bus to
Knockholt Pound from Orpington**

**Head up and over the North Downs for
some long views northwards to London
and southwards into Kent.**

The walk starts from the centre of the
village of Knockholt Pound at the
junction of Harrow Road with Chevening
Lane by The Three Horseshoes pub. The
pub dates back to at least the 18th century
and stands on an old drovers' route, at the
meeting of five roads. As the name of the
village suggests, there used to be a pound
for animals here and Knockholt probably
means 'the oak copse' in Old English.

To the west of the village, visible just
off the route, are Knockholt Beeches,
locally famous for being the highest point
of the highest village in Kent and, as

legend has it, the spot was even visited
by William the Conqueror. The walk
also passes through the parkland of
Chevening House, once the country seat
of the Lennard and then Stanhope
families. In the 20th century the house
and grounds were bequeathed to the
nation and are now a government
country residence.

Walk up Chevening Lane past houses
for just over 500m to the top and take the
North Downs Way off right along the
edges of four fields with a view to the
right over London – in the second field
you pass a memorial to the guidebook
writer Roland Oakeley, in the third field
the North Downs Way bends to the right
and at the end of the fourth it turns left
into Cooper's Wood. Head through the
trees, where the North Downs Way
doglegs briefly left, then right to a field
and along its left edge to Sundridge Lane.

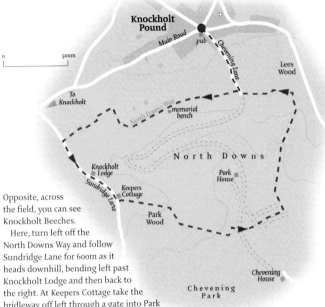

Opposite, across the field, you can see Knockholt Beeches.

Here, turn left off the North Downs Way and follow Sundridge Lane for 600m as it heads downhill, bending left past Knockholt Lodge and then back to the right. At Keepers Cottage take the bridleway off left through a gate into Park Wood. After just over 150m the bridleway becomes a footpath and in another 200m it veers to the right, down to the wood's southern edge and a handy bench for taking in the view.

The route now bears left into fields and down alongside the wood, with a long view out over Chevening Park and House. The footpath bends left around the bottom edge of the wood, before turning right and following the fence and well-signed route over the parkland and across the driveway of Chevening House. Continue to the trees ahead, where the footpath doglegs briefly left, then right over a second driveway and along the fence to the corner of the wood ahead.

Here, turn left along the edge of the wood to a gate into a field. The route now bears to the right and heads up the increasingly steep coombe to a stile into woodland. It's worth pausing here to take in the view back over the parkland. Continue up through the woodland and into the field beyond to the junction with the North Downs Way. Follow the North Downs Way as it now turns left through Lees Wood and then along a field edge to the top of Chevening Lane again, where a right turn will take you back to the start.

◀ Looking southwestwards over Chevening Park

Westerham and Chartwell

Distance 7.5km **Time** 2 hours 15
Terrain woodland paths and fields
Map OS Explorer 147 **Access** bus to
Westerham from Sevenoaks, Tonbridge
and Oxted

**Enjoy an undulating walk over fields and
through woodlands, with the option of
visiting Chartwell.**

Westerham is closely associated with Sir
Winston Churchill and nearby Chartwell,
his private residence, which can be visited
along the route. Churchill restored the
house and gardens in the 1920s and the
National Trust acquired them in 1946. On
The Green in the centre of Westerham is a
bronze statue of a seated Churchill. At the
other end is the equally imposing statue
of Major-General James Wolfe, who was
born in Westerham in 1727 and died at the
Battle of Quebec in 1759. The National
Trust also owns Quebec House, Wolfe's
childhood home in Westerham, and
St Mary's Church has a memorial window
dedicated to him. The town's main Darent
car park is situated on the eastern edge of
Westerham with signs to the town centre.

From The Green in Westerham cross the
A25 and head up steps along Water Lane
down to a gate into fields. Turn right
along the bottom of the field, cross the
River Darent and turn left with the
Greensand Way along Mill Lane up past
Park Lodge. Continue uphill along a
fenced path and over fields to a gate. Keep
on into the trees, over a track and up
through the woodland for just under 1km.
At the high point ignore a Greensand Way
permissive path off right and keep ahead
for 200m down to the sharp left-hand
bend by Kent Hatch Lodge.

Westerham

To Sevenoaks

River Darent

A25

To Oxted

Park Lodge

Glebe House

Squerryes Court

Hosey Hill

Greensand Way

Squerryes Park

HOSEY COMMON

Tower Wood

B2026

Goodley Stock Road

Horns Hill

Goodley Stock

Kent Hatch Lodge

Hosey Common Rd

car park

Chartwell

B269

Kent Hatch

Crockhamhill Common

April Cottage

Mariners Hill

0 _____ 1km

The Greensand Way forks right off the track, past the lodge and along its driveway for 75m to a bridleway junction just before the road. Turn left uphill with the Way and cross the next bridleway junction. In another 50m the Greensand Way forks left and then, 100m further on, right onto a footpath over Crockhamhill Common for 250m to a path junction. Dogleg right to the driveway, then left to stay on the Greensand Way, which immediately forks left off the driveway onto a footpath back into the trees. Continue gently uphill and round to the left to a house in a clearing. Keep on past the house over the high point of the common and descend to a bridleway junction by April Cottage. Turn right up to and across Hosey Common Road, where the Greensand Way climbs steeply for 100m before levelling out and forking left onto a footpath over the top of Mariners Hill. From here, walk down to the road opposite the entrance to Chartwell, whose tearooms are accessible through the car park.

The return route follows the National Trust's Chartwell to Westerham Trail initially along a fenced path and then steeply up and across a lane. The waymarked trail then guides you down through woodland, bending left to a path junction. Here, turn left down Hosey Common for just under 1km towards a car park. Just before the car park, turn left across Hosey Common Road and go left onto a footpath along the edge of woodland. Continue down to a footpath junction in Tower Wood and turn right to a path junction at the edge of the wood. Here, fork right steeply up the grassy slope and over the field beyond. At the marker post in the middle, bear half-left down through a gate and the steep field beyond to reach the bottom of Water Lane again, which takes you back to the start.

◀ The statue of Winston Churchill on The Green, Westerham

Toy's Hill and Ide Hill

Distance **7.5km** Time **2 hours 15**
Terrain **woodland and fields, with two
steep ascents** Map **OS Explorer 147**
Access **no public transport to the start**

**This varied up-and-down route takes you
on and below the Greensand Ridge.**

The walk starts from the Toy's Hill
National Trust car park on Chart Lane,
400m north of Toy's Hill. Cross Chart Lane
and head into woodland along the
Greensand Way, which forks left after 30m
gently downhill to a six-way path
junction. The Greensand Way bends to the
right here (ignore the two paths off sharp
right) and descends more steeply, down
over a bridleway junction to the bottom of
Scords Wood into fields.

Bear left down two fields, across a
footbridge over a stream, and then climb
the far side of the valley up three more
fields to the houses of Ide Hill and along a
lane to Sundridge Road. Here, a right turn
takes you past the small roundabout and
up beside The Green, off the route of the
Greensand Way, and past St Mary's
Church. Beyond the last house, bear left
into woodland, up over a small rise and
then down and to the left. Follow the
contouring path through the trees for
150m before cutting back to the right
down to Ide Hill Road, the B2042. On the
left is a car park and Ide Hill Community
Shop and Post Office, which has a small
café and a long view down to Bough
Beech Reservoir.

Go left past the car park back onto the
route of the Greensand Way and, at the
left-hand bend beyond, cross Ide Hill
Road and head down Hanging Bank lane,
where the Greensand Way immediately
forks left up a track. After 150m, at the
path junction where the Greensand Way
turns sharp left, keep ahead past Quarry
Cottage and descend the bridleway to
rejoin the lane. Turn left, down round the

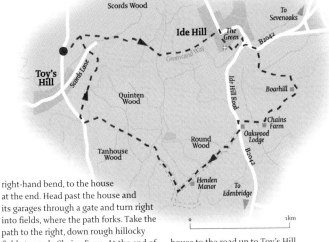

Scords Wood

Ide Hill

The Green

To Sevenoaks

B2042

Toy's Hill

Scords Lane

Greensand Way

Ide Hill Road

Boarhill

Quinten Wood

Chains Farm

Oakwood Lodge

Round Wood

B2042

Tanhouse Wood

Henden Manor

To Edenbridge

0   1km

right-hand bend, to the house at the end. Head past the house and its garages through a gate and turn right into fields, where the path forks. Take the path to the right, down rough hillocky fields towards Chains Farm. At the end of the third field bear right through a gate, past the farmhouse and along the track up to Ide Hill Road.

Turn left along the verge for 75m past Oakwood Lodge and then right across the road onto the footpath leading down the driveway to Henden Manor for 600m. Keep on past the manor house, farm buildings and the Oast House and continue up the drive beyond for 100m to a junction by semi-detached houses. Turn right onto a footpath, along a concrete track for 350m, through a gate and then along a gravel track, which soon bends left down past a wood into fields. Follow the right-hand edge of the first two fields to a gate by the corner of woodland. Head diagonally up the field beyond and through a line of oaks to a gate at the top, where a left turn takes you beside a garden and

house to the road up to Toy's Hill.

Go right up the road for 75m and take the footpath off right back into fields. The path heads over the shoulder of the hill and contours over two fields below houses and gardens to a gate on the far side. The footpath continues up past houses and then through the gate to Clyvers House, beyond which it passes along a fenced section between gardens and soon bends sharp left, climbing steeply up a narrow pathway to emerge onto a lane. Now bear left uphill to the junction with Scords Lane and take the footpath ahead up steps into Scords Wood again. The path climbs very steeply before the gradient eases and you reach the six-way path junction on the Greensand Way, passed on the outward route. Turn left to retrace steps back along the Greensand Way to Toy's Hill car park.

◀ The view south from Ide Hill

Sevenoaks and Knole Park

Distance 6.5km Time 1 hour 30
Terrain parkland paths
Map OS Explorer 147 Access bus to
Sevenoaks from Tonbridge, Tunbridge
Wells and Maidstone; train from London,
Tonbridge and Tunbridge Wells

An extended parkland stroll follows
tree-lined walks with the option to visit
world-famous Knole itself.

Knole is just a short walk from the
centre of Sevenoaks and was originally
built as an archbishop's palace and passed
through the ownership of kings and
queens, including Elizabeth I and Henry
VIII, to the Sackville family. The National
Trust now owns the house. The extensive
deer park covers many hundreds of acres
of woodland, valleys and parkland with a
number of grand walkways and avenues.
Lining these walks can be found
magnificent veteran trees, some dating to
the 1700s. You are also likely to spot

plenty of wild deer, both sika and fallow
varieties. There is the option to visit the
main house and the Brewhouse Café is
open to all.

The walk starts from the High Street in
Sevenoaks, opposite St Nicholas Church.
Go through the main entrance to Knole
Park and walk down the hill to the gates
and ticket booth. Pedestrians can enter
the park for free. Dogs must be on a lead.
The walk, in part, follows the park's family
route (red waymarks) with an extension
over Knole Park Golf Course.

Pass through the pedestrian gate beside
the cattle grid and head down the
driveway to the bottom of the dip. Fork
right uphill off the driveway and then bear
right with the Greensand Way, which
heads past the icehouse towards the
corner of the main house. From here
continue along the waymarked red-route
path to the right of the main house and
then parallel with the walled garden for

◄ Knole's northern façade

400m on a broad sandy path. Where the wall ends, continue ahead for another 250m to the junction with Broad Walk.

A right turn takes you up the straight walk for 1km, between trees to the high point and the junction with Chestnut Walk. The route here turns sharp left along Chestnut Walk for a further 1km. The sheer number of chestnut trees lining the walk is impressive, as well as the shapes and size of the oldest ones. After 1km the waymarked red route heads off left, back down to the main house, but you can extend the walk by continuing along Chestnut Walk for another 400m.

At the end of the walk turn left and follow the public footpath along the driveway down past Keepers Cottage and its pond. Beyond, the driveway swings to the right and then back left down into a dip – watch out for golfers here as you start to cross the golf course. A little way up the far side of the dip, leave the driveway and follow the well-waymarked footpath up over the rise and round a little to the left over the fairways for 500m to reach the main house's northern side. Here, you will find the entrance to the Brewhouse Café. At the front of the house, bear left through the car park and, where the car park driveway turns right, keep ahead to rejoin the outward path back down across the dip and up through the entrance gates to the High Street.

Shipbourne and Ightham Mote

Distance **5km** Time **1 hour 30**
Terrain **fields, woodland and lanes**
Map **OS Explorer 147** Access **bus to
Shipbourne from Wrotham, Tunbridge
Wells and Tonbridge**

**Amble over rolling countryside with long
views and the chance to visit a glorious
moated manor house.**

The walk starts in the village of
Shipbourne by the Church of St Giles, at
the junction of the A227 with Upper Green
Road, a little way along which there is a
parking lay-by on the common. It's worth
looking inside the church for its
impressive and unusual interior *sgraffito*
decoration on the walls of the nave, where
the top layer of white plaster has been
scratched through to reveal the striking
red and black underlayers. There are also
some touching memorials to the families
who have owned nearby Fairlawne – the

Cazalets and, before them, the Vanes.

Also on the route is Ightham Mote, the
famous 14th-century moated manor
house. This came into the possession of
the National Trust in 1985 and it has since
restored and rebuilt much of the original
building. The architectural historian
Sir Nikolaus Pevsner called it 'the most
complete small medieval manor house in
the county'. The house and gardens are
open to the visiting public, and the
tearooms are accessible to all.

Walk past the church to the far end of
the churchyard, where there is a three-way
path junction, marked by a fingerpost.
Take the footpath off right over the stile
on the Greensand Way, which is followed
for the first half of the walk. Head over the
grass area and driveway and then along
the right-hand edge of two fields and into
the third field, where the footpath forks.
Bear left with the Greensand Way, which

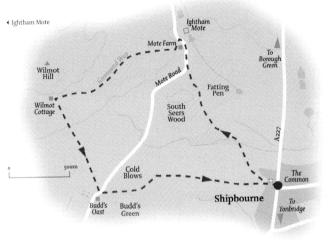

◄ Ightham Mote

heads alongside trees and then curves up to the right into woodland.

The footpath, now fenced, continues uphill through the trees, over the rise and down out of the wood, before passing along the edges of two more fields to a lane. Turn right up the lane past Mote Farmhouse to the left-hand bend, where you can detour off right to Ightham Mote to visit the house itself or just the tearooms – head down the drive, bear right past the house and up round the left-hand bend.

The onward route continues round the bend and then turns left with the Greensand Way up to Mote Farm. Continue past the farm buildings and bend right with the track, which now climbs steadily between fields for 500m up to a bridleway junction at the high point. Here, the Greensand Way carries straight on down through woodland, before heading fairly steeply uphill again, with good views left over the Weald, to a path junction by Wilmot Cottage.

You now leave the Greensand Way and turn left through a gate and down the edges of four fields to Mote Road. A short dogleg right, then left over the road by Budd's Oast leads onto a footpath which rises up through a conifer plantation and then deciduous woodland. After 400m you bend left over the top of the rise and down to a footpath junction at the far edge of the wood. A right turn takes you gently down a wide footpath just inside the wood for 200m to a stile into fields. From here, continue ahead over two fields, with the Church of St Giles to guide you back to the start.

Edenbridge and the River Eden

Distance 6.5km **Time** 1 hour 45
Terrain fields and riverside paths, prone
to flooding and muddy in winter
Map OS Explorer 147 **Access** bus to
**Edenbridge from Tunbridge Wells, East
Grinstead and Oxted; train to Edenbridge
Town Station from London Bridge and
Oxted and to Edenbridge Station (1.5km
north of the town centre) from Tonbridge
and Redhill**

**Border-hop your way over the meadows
and fields of the Eden Valley on a
delightful walk that's mostly level.**

Edenbridge sits near the county border
with Surrey and the many wooden-
framed buildings in the town give an
immediate sense of its long history.
The Eden Valley Museum on the High
Street outlines the area's past and
contains collections and displays of
artefacts on the social history and
archaeology of the town and the Eden
Valley, including the Chiddingstone

Hoard. In 2018 the museum raised
sufficient funds to purchase the hoard
of 10 gold coins which had been found by
a local metal-detectorist. Later assessment
at the British Museum established that
the coins had been minted in the middle
of the 1st century BCE in Gaul, at the time
threatened by Roman invasion, and
probably brought to Britain as payment or
gifts for local tribal leaders. The coins are
now on permanent display.

From the High Street in Edenbridge,
just up from the Eden Valley Museum and
opposite the walkway to Market Yard car
park, head along Lingfield Road and cross
over Mont St Aignan Way, named after the
twinned town in Normandy. Continue
along Lingfield Road past houses for
200m on the Eden Valley Walk, which is
followed for the first half of the route, and
turn left along Coomb Field road to the
playing field. The Eden Valley Walk heads
around the left-hand side of the sports
pitches beside the tree-lined Mill Race and

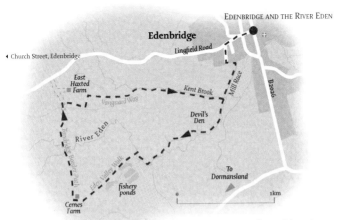

Edenbridge

Lingfield Road

◄ Church Street, Edenbridge

East
Haxted
Farm

Kent Brook

Mill Race

B2026

Vanguard Way

Devil's
Den

River Eden

Eden Valley Walk

fishery
ponds

To
Dormansland

Cernes
Farm

0   1km

across the footbridge over the Kent Brook.

Keep ahead, now alongside the River Eden, over the riverside fields. The Eden Valley Walk soon bends right with the river to the wooded and moated Devil's Den. The Eden Valley Walk leaves the River Eden here and follows the edges of two more fields alongside a ditch before crossing left over the ditch (you pass a sign here to be alert for light aircraft landing on the grassy airstrip) and across the field beyond, past a pillbox, to reach the river again. The path now bears to the right beside the river and soon bends right to an area of scrubby woodland.

Here, the Eden Valley Walk turns left over the River Eden and the county border with Surrey, across the field beyond and along a wooded track for 100m. At the bend keep ahead past Gabriels Fishery ponds and over a track junction into fields. Head across Cernes Field and in the second field fork right, off the Eden Valley Walk, to the track by the entrance to Cernes Farm.

You now cross over the track into the field beyond and turn right with the Vanguard Way over a series of five fields and two footbridges back across the River Eden. Head over the field beyond and up through some scrubby woodland and along a fenced path to reach a fingerpost below East Haxted Farm. The Vanguard Way turns right and passes below the timber-framed farmhouse along the field edge before turning left up the next field to the top of the rise. Here, turn right over the top of the field and down a smaller second field. Just before the hedge at the bottom the Vanguard Way doglegs left to the Kent Brook and then right to continue alongside it.

After 100m the Vanguard Way heads off left over the brook, but the return route continues alongside it for another 800m along field edges and through a woodland of young oak trees to reach the River Eden again. Turn left back over the Kent Brook and retrace steps over the playing field and along Lingfield Road into Edenbridge.

Chiddingstone and Hever

Distance 9km **Time** 2 hours
Terrain lanes, fields and woodland
Map OS Explorer 147 **Access** no public
transport to the start

This walk is brimming with history, with two villages and their castles and churches to explore.

Chiddingstone is known for its High Street of Tudor buildings and its castle, which along with its grounds is open to the public. St Mary's Church is also worth a visit, especially to see one of the few surviving 18th-century 'vinegar' bibles, so-called because of their misspelling of 'vineyard' as 'vinegar' in St Luke's gospel. You can also detour to the Chiding Stone, a large sandstone mass with Druidical associations. Along the route there is also Hever Church, which contains the tomb of Sir Thomas Bullen, grandfather of Elizabeth I and father of Anne Boleyn, whose childhood home was Hever Castle.

Walk up the High Street past the school and the path to the Chiding Stone. Opposite Glebe House, turn right up a footpath and at the top continue across the field beyond down to a gate and crosspaths. Turn right through a small wood and carry on over two fields, where the Eden Valley Walk joins from the left and is followed to Hever. At the houses of Hill Hoath dogleg right down a track for 50m, then left past more houses to a gate. Continue along the bridleway up into woodland, over the rise and down to a fork in the path, where a marker post points the way off right into Moor Wood.

Drop through the wood to a footbridge over a stream, dogleg right along the edge of a field and then left up to a lane. The Eden Valley Walk continues across the lane, up between trees and past houses to a track junction by Bothy Cottage.

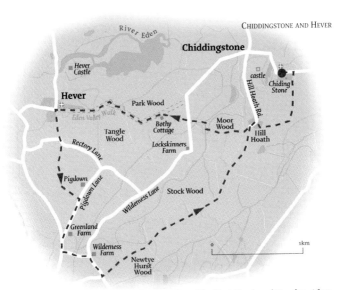

Keep ahead on the Eden Valley Walk on a grassy track alongside a driveway and round the right bend. The footpath joins the driveway down through some bends in woodland to a lane junction. Turn left along a fenced-off path parallel with the lane for 500m and through the churchyard of Hever Church to the road. The entrance to Hever Castle is off to the right.

Turn left and, at the bend, leave the Eden Valley Walk and keep ahead onto a footpath past the primary school and through woodland to a lane. Bear left along the lane for 30m and at the bend fork right up into fields. Bear left along the left-hand edge of three fields to a footpath junction at the start of the fourth. Here, fork left up the fenced path to Pigdown Lane. Turn right up the lane to the junction, then left along the road,

signed for Mark Beech and Cowden. After 100m go left along Dyehurst Lane through the bends up to a junction opposite Wilderness Farm, then turn right up to the next junction.

Here, turn left through a gate onto the footpath through Newtye Hurst Wood down to a gate at its far edge. The route now continues between fields, over a crosstrack and alongside a wood on the right, before passing over a rise between more fields to a gate into Stock Wood. The path descends gently through the wood, bends left and passes along a fenced section to a gate. Bear to the right here down a long field to a gate at the bottom. Just beyond the gate, turn right onto the Eden Valley Walk and retrace the outward route up through Hill Hoath and back to Chiddingstone.

◀ The approach to Chiddingstone Castle from the south

Penshurst Park

Distance **4.5km** Time **1 hour 15**
Terrain **parkland and fields, with one
gentle climb** Map **OS Explorer 147**
Access **bus to Penshurst from Edenbridge
and Tunbridge Wells**

**An elegant parkland stroll gives long
views back over Penshurst Place and the
surrounding countryside.**

The walk crosses the parkland of
Penshurst Place, whose original buildings
date from the 14th century and in the
16th century became the ancestral home
of the Sidney family. One of the family's
most famous members born at Penshurst
is Sir Philip Sidney, the Elizabethan
statesman, soldier and poet. He is perhaps
best known nowadays for his pastoral
romance *Arcadia*, in one part of which he
praises the exquisite setting of his home.

From the High Street in Penshurst
village walk past The Leicester Arms on
the right and then Leicester Square on
the left, with its pathway through to the
Church of St John the Baptist, to the
arched gateway to the Penshurst Estate.
The route initially follows the Eden Valley
Walk, which heads through the gateway
and down the driveway for 800m,
alongside the wall of the house, its
parkland and then fields. Just beyond the
second of two ponds follow the Eden
Valley Walk as it bears left into fields and
along the right-hand edge of the first field
to a gate, before climbing up the slope in
the second field to the hedge at the top.

Here, you leave the Eden Valley Walk,
which continues ahead, and turn left
along the top of the field, with the hedge
on your right, to a gate. The footpath

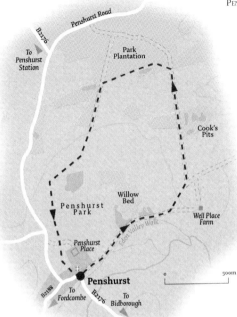

continues ahead for 800m along a straight tree-lined track, passing between two stands of woodland and rising gently to a footpath junction at the trees ahead. You now turn left and follow the footpath along a wide grassy strip along an avenue of plane trees for 500m, with a plantation over to the right and views down over Penshurst Park to the left. On reaching a path junction marked by a fingerpost at the end of the avenue just before a wood, turn left down a broad track between trees to a gate.

Go through the gate and follow the footpath which leads a little to the right of a line of oak trees over the parkland to a second gate. Continue ahead along the left-hand field edge and pass the lake, with Penshurst Place visible beyond. After another 100m the footpath turns left through a third gate and heads across the parkland and over a driveway, before passing to the right of Penshurst Place itself to a gate to the church. Go through the churchyard past the church, which has a rare dole table by the south door and, inside, the Sidney Chapel, known for its decorated ceiling. Continue through Leicester Square with its wooden Guildhouse to return to the village centre.

Closest to London, and often bypassed in a triangle of motorways, lies the still tranquil Darent Valley, where the famous Roman villa at Lullingstone was unearthed and is now surrounded by its own country park. Just north of the M20, near its junction with the M26, the slopes of the North Downs extend above Trottiscliffe, only to be breached north of Maidstone by the lower reaches of the River Medway and its tidal estuary beyond. Here, the Hoo Peninsula and, on the estuary's eastern side, the Isle of Sheppey extend in an expanse of marshland and low-lying fields, with holiday resorts, wildlife reserves and estuarine industries looking out over the waters of the Thames Estuary. The Medway towns of Rochester, Chatham and Gillingham, along with Sittingbourne and Faversham further to the east, were once among the most important commercial ports and military bases in the country. Inland, and to the south of the M2 motorway, lies a scattering of North Downs villages and hamlets, still set amongst fields, orchards and woodland.

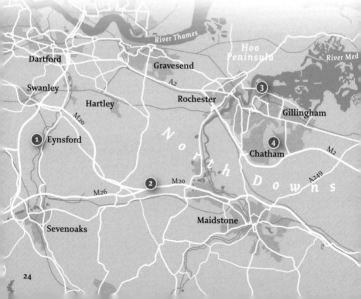

Swanley to Faversham

Sheerness

Leysdown-on-Sea

Isle of Sheppey   **6**

Sittingbourne
A2

7

Faversham

5

8

Challock

Lullingstone Country Park

Distance 6.5km **Time** 1 hour 45
Terrain fields, lanes, woodland and paths
over golf course fairways
Maps OS Explorer 147 & 162 **Access** bus to
Lullingstone Country Park (request stop)
from Sevenoaks and Swanley

Enjoy an undulating route in the secluded Darent Valley with the option of visiting a castle and a Roman villa.

The walk starts from Lullingstone Country Park Visitor Centre, located in the Darent Valley between Eynsford and Shoreham, where there is a car park, a café and a play area for younger children, as well as picnic tables. The park itself covers more than 450 acres of chalk grassland and ancient woodlands and offers three waymarked trails. This walk follows the longest one, called the Lullingstone Loop, which is waymarked with black arrows.

Along the route you pass the entrance to Lullingstone Castle, whose family mansion and gardens are open to the public on certain days, and Lullingstone Roman Villa, one of a number in this part of the county constructed in the 1st century CE. The Lullingstone Villa site is now managed by English Heritage and is covered by a specially-designed structure to preserve the remains. This villa is notable for its well-preserved mosaics and a room used as a pagan shrine and later as a Christian chapel, thought to be one of the earliest of its kind in Britain.

Go past the entrance to the visitor centre and its café and turn right by the small play area to the River Darent. A left turn takes you onto the riverside path for 500m to a weir. Keep ahead to the entrance to Lullingstone Castle and along the lane for another 600m towards Lullingstone Roman Villa.

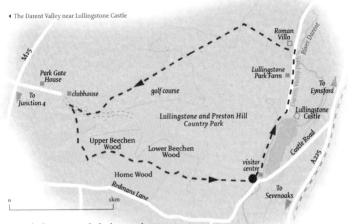

◀ The Darent Valley near Lullingstone Castle

Just before you reach the low modern building covering the remains of the Roman villa, the loop turns left up steps through woodland into fields. Head up the left-hand edge of the first field and into the second, where the path bears left through the line of trees and then up across the middle of the field beyond, over the rise and down past a path junction into the dip. Keep ahead uphill through the trees and then along the edge of a field, forking left to reach a strip of woodland.

The path continues just inside the edge of the trees for 600m, with golf course fairways on the left and then on the right. At the far end of the wood you come to a junction with a golf course driveway. Fork right along the driveway and head round the right-hand bend

for 75m. About 100m before the clubhouse, look out for the marker post as the loop turns sharp left onto a footpath which heads down through the trees, across a fairway – watch out for golfers on the right – and then back into trees, before climbing up the far side of the valley to the top edge of the wood.

The Lullingstone Loop now turns left along the woodland edge and in 200m you'll need to take the right fork in the path, which soon heads down across a small clearing in a dip and up the far side to a gate. From here, follow signs for the visitor centre for the final 800m, down alongside the edge of the wood and then beside a fence back to the car park and the start.

Trosley and Coldrum Long Barrow

Distance 6km **Time** 1 hour 30
Terrain woodland and fields with one
steep climb **Map** OS Explorer 148
Access bus to Vigo Village from Bluewater
and Sevenoaks (Monday to Friday)

**There are plenty of woodland surprises
on this walk along the North Downs Way
before a descent takes you to a Neolithic
burial chamber.**

The walk starts from Trosley Country
Park, situated near Vigo Village between
Wrotham and Meopham off the A227,
where there is a car park and visitor centre
with a café and toilets. The park is popular
with dog walkers, runners, horse riders
and ramblers and comprises a mix of
woodland and chalk downland. There is
also a woodland play area for younger
children, a Woodland Orchestra and a
Wood Henge art installation. There is even
a trim trail with 10 exercise stations. This
route heads through the woodland before
descending the downland escarpment to

Coldrum Long Barrow, a Neolithic burial
chamber originally covered by a mound
and surrounded by standing sarsen
stones. The name Coldrum was taken
from a nearby farm. Further along the
route, you also pass by the site of a
recently-discovered Roman villa and
bathhouse complex.

From the car park walk past the visitor
centre and head down to the right to the
path junction with the North Downs Way.
Bend round to the left to join the North
Downs Way, which heads through Downs
Wood for the next 1.5km on a mostly level
path, where you can pause at various
viewpoints and investigate the Woodland
Orchestra and, further on, the sculptures
of the Wood Henge art installation. Keep
on past the path down to Quarry Field,
after which the North Downs Way bends
left and climbs to meet a byway.

A sharp right turn takes you down the
steep stony byway to a track junction by
houses at the bottom of the wood. Leave

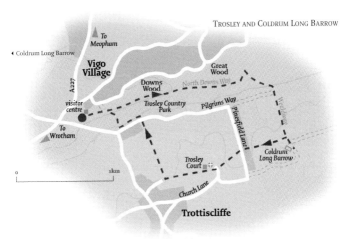

To Meopham

◄ Coldrum Long Barrow

Vigo Village

Great Wood

Downs Wood

North Downs Way

A227

visitor centre

Trosley Country Park

Pilgrims Way

Wealdway

To Wrotham

Pinesfield Lane

Coldrum Long Barrow

Trosley Court

0   1km

Church Lane

Trottiscliffe

the North Downs Way here as it heads off to the left, and join the Wealdway. Follow the track round the right bend and turn immediately left, signed for Coldrum Long Barrow, down alongside a field to a junction with a bridleway. From here, carry on along the path for another 100m to Coldrum Long Barrow.

The return route retraces steps to the bridleway junction and turns left up over a field and down through woodland. You now head up a driveway track, through a gate and past a small parking area to reach a lane. Continue over the lane, across the field beyond and down past a house, where a right turn takes you past the small Church of St Peter and St Paul to Trosley Court.

Here, keep ahead on the bridleway through the buildings of Trosley Court and along the left-hand edge of the field beyond, where just on the right in the summer of 2022 the remains of a Roman bathhouse and villa complex were

unearthed by Kent Archaeological Society. The week-long excavations revealed a hypocaust system, sherds of blackware and red pottery, tiles, squared bricks, the foundations of solid masonry walls and an area of debris caused by collapse or demolition. The complex is located on the ancient spring-line, as are a number of other Roman settlements in the area, including nearby Lullingstone Villa. Further excavations are planned to reveal more of the site.

Continue to the houses on the far side and turn right up the field to the lane at the top. Cross over the lane and into the wood a little way before turning left onto the path, which leads alongside a wire fence parallel with the lane before turning right steeply up steps. The waymarked footpath soon bends to the left and continues uphill less steeply to reach the junction with the North Downs Way, where a left turn will take you back to the start.

Upnor and Hoo St Werburgh

Distance 8.5km **Time** 2 hours 15
Terrain lanes, fields and tidal shoreline,
which can be inaccessible during high
tide **Map** OS Explorer 163 **Access** bus to
Upnor from Chatham and Rochester

**Meander through the modern marinas
alongside the River Medway on a walk
brimming with maritime history.**

The walk starts at Upper Upnor, situated
north of Chatham and Rochester beside
the River Medway at the southern end of
the Hoo Peninsula, where there is a car
park. One section of the outward route
passes along the shoreline, sections of
which can be inaccessible at high tide. If
high tide times are not convenient, an
alternative might be to start from Hoo
St Werburgh. The Hoo Peninsula extends
northwards and eastwards between the
Thames Estuary and the River Medway
and traces its name from a Saxon word
which itself means a 'spur of land'. On the
peninsula, marshes and farmland exist
side by side with heavy industry and
power stations and there is a long military

association with the Royal Dockyards at
nearby Chatham.

The route follows the Saxon Shore Way,
which is well-waymarked. It is worth
making a short detour to the bottom of
the narrow cobbled High Street in Upper
Upnor for the view across the River
Medway by the entrance to Upnor Castle,
an artillery fort built in the 16th century
to protect Chatham Dockyard opposite.

From the top of the High Street head up
Upchat Road to the bend and bear right
with the Saxon Shore Way on a tarmac
path alongside the perimeter wall of
Upnor Castle for 300m and down steps to
Upnor Road. Turn right through Lower
Upnor past Ordnance Yard and some
modern housing to The Ship tavern and
Upnor Sailing Club. Just beyond, the
Saxon Shore Way forks right to stay
beside the River Medway and passes two
London Stones. These were originally set
up at the limits of the City of London's
control over the River Medway. The larger
newer stone, made of granite and dated
1836, is located in front of the smaller

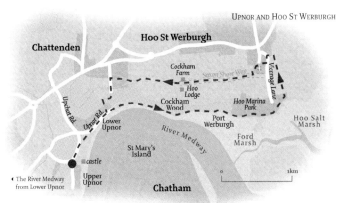

The River Medway from Lower Upnor

older one. From the stones, go past Lower Upnor car park and Medway Yacht Club.

The Saxon Shore Way now heads along the shoreline at the foot of Cockham Wood for the next 1.5km, where sections can be muddy and also covered at high tide, past Wilsonian Sailing Club on a small promontory and then past the red-brick ruin of Cockham Wood Fort before reaching Port Werburgh. There is plenty to see on this part of the walk – old slipways, moored boats, wrecked hulls – and, if the tide allows the time, it's a good place for bird-spotting and beachcombing.

Carry on following the well-signed route for the next 1km through Hoo Marina past the moorings, boatyards and yacht clubs and then alongside the tall fence of the marina – this section is very much a working marina, but there is plenty of interest among the houseboats, yachts and boatyards. When you reach the gates of Stargate Marine, turn left through a small private parking area and continue along the Saxon Shore Way into fields, where the spire of Hoo St Werburgh

Church is visible ahead and to the left. At the end of the fields, turn left along the road past houses to the junction. The Saxon Shore Way doglegs left for 100m along Vicarage Lane and then right onto a footpath through the graveyard to Hoo St Werburgh Parish Church. From here, you can detour off right along Church Street for 200m to local shops and pubs.

The onward route leads out of the far end of the graveyard along a fenced path between houses to a field and turns left to reach a byway. Go right along the tarmac byway and follow it for the next 1km up between fields to Cockham Farm and Hoo Lodge. The byway, now a track, continues westwards between fields for another 1km and then passes between houses along a fenced pathway to reach Elm Avenue. Turn left up past houses to the top of the road, where the Saxon Shore Way continues ahead onto a footpath down into woodland, before making a broad dogleg to the right and then left back down into Lower Upnor. From here, retrace the outward route to the start.

31

Capstone Farm Country Park

Distance **3.25km** Time **1 hour**
Terrain **woodland paths and fields**
Map **OS Explorer 163** Access **no public
transport to the start**

**The woods and fields of an old farm are
the setting for a gentle but varied stroll.**

Capstone Farm Country Park is situated
on the southern edge of Gillingham and
covers an area of former farmland on the
North Downs, with a mix of ancient
woodland, old orchards, chalk grassland
and a freshwater lake, as well as a
children's play area. Until the late 20th
century Capstone was a working farm,
with the area now occupied by the lake
used for growing hops, and there had
been farming on the site for at least 700
years. In 1984 the park was opened to the
public and is now managed by Medway
Council. There is also a visitor centre and

a small café by the lake. Entrance to the
park, along with its car park, is free.

There are four waymarked routes
around the park. This walk follows the
Green Trail which the Park advises is
suitable for the intermediate walker and
takes you along the front of the park
toward Drow Hill, round the old cherry
orchard, through Drow Hill Woods and
back down valley fields and through its
Millennium Wood.

From the visitor centre by the lake, head
up through a small parking area and
follow the marker arrows up to the left
and round the bend to the top of the
children's play area. The Green Trail forks
right up the bank and then heads half-left
along a path into the trees above the main
car parks and down to Capstone Road,
before heading parallel with the road up
past the ski centre. Turn right up the

◄ The lake in Capstone Farm Country Park

access road and continue ahead on the path parallel to it up Drow Hill towards Orchard car park.

Before reaching the car park the Green Trail turns left across the access road into woodland, where it twists its way through the trees before turning right uphill to a path junction to the rear of Orchard car park. Bear left here through Drow Hill Wood, where the winding path gradually bends to the right to reach a brick pavilion at the far edge of the wood.

The Green Trail now heads left past the pavilion and across an open area towards a hedge, before turning right to a marker post by the trees on the far side and then right again alongside them to bring you

back parallel with the pavilion. You now turn left through trees down to a path junction in a shallow valley. Here, turn right and head down the valley field and, at the trees ahead, turn left and follow the path along the edge of the trees as it bends round to the right. You soon start descending on a grassy path alongside a hedge and then down the edge of Millennium Wood to reach the bank just above the children's play area once again, with the lake and visitor centre back down to the left.

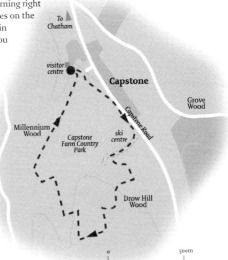

Newnham and Doddington

Distance 8.5km **Time** 2 hours 15
Terrain lanes, woodland and fields
Map OS Explorer 149 **Access** bus to
Newnham from Sittingbourne

**Delve into the history of three charming
villages on a gentle ramble through
woods and over undulating farmland.**

Newnham is known for its 13th-century
church and the unusual Calico House,
which in origin was a medieval hall house
but in the 18th century saw its frontage
decorated in red and white plaster in the
style of calico fabric. Eastling is an ancient
village and may well date to the 5th
century when the tribe of the Eslinges
were settled here, close to the ancient
trackway which runs nearby. In the
churchyard there is a large yew, certified
to be 2000 years old. The last village along
the route, Doddington, is unusual in
having a parish church dedicated to the
Decollation (beheading) of St John the
Baptist, and is the only one of its kind in
Kent. This dedication gives considerable
support to the theory that located here
was a very rare medieval holy relic, none
other than the stone on which John the
Baptist was put to death. This stone was
brought to England in the 14th century
and finally ended up in nearby Charing.

From the centre of Newnham by the
Church of St Peter and St Paul walk
through the village along the road
towards Faversham and in 200m, just
before the last house, take the footpath
off to the right. The footpath leads uphill
into woodland to the top of the rise and
passes along a track for 100m on the edge
of a clearing to a path junction. The route
follows the left fork downhill through the
trees again into a shallow dip, before
heading uphill just inside the edge of the
wood for another 400m to reach Eastling
Road. Turn right along the pavement past
the modern Glebe Cottages and the
junction with Newnham Lane, beyond
which you can detour along the field path
on the left to see the Church of St Mary.
From the centre of Eastling, by The

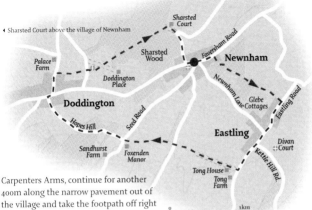

◀ Sharsted Court above the village of Newnham

Carpenters Arms, continue for another 400m along the narrow pavement out of the village and take the footpath off right to Tong Farm.

The route now heads along the track past the black-timbered and white-plastered frontage of Tong House and over a series of five fields in the direction of Seed – where the track bends left at the end of the first field, keep ahead down across the dip in the second field and over the middle of the third to a lane; a quick dogleg left, then right over the lane takes you across a larger dip in the fourth field and then finally up over the fifth and along the left-hand edge of an orchard to Seed. Cross Seed Road and take the lane opposite for the next 1.2km, signed for Doddington. Hopes Hill is a delightful narrow lane which leads downhill into woodland and twists its way down and up over two dips before passing over a final rise to take you down to Doddington.

At the road junction dogleg right into the village, then left up Chequers Hill, past The Chequers Inn, and head steeply uphill for 200m. Just before the last house take

the footpath off right along the right-hand field edge, through a stand of beech trees and over the lane by the Church of the Beheading of St John the Baptist, which has an unusual clapboard tower. The original medieval one had been struck by lightning in the 17th century and was dismantled in the 19th century. Inside are some 13th-century wall-paintings, one of which has been identified as St Francis receiving the stigmata.

At the far end of the churchyard, at the path junction, fork left and follow the waymarks across the parkland of Doddington Place and then through Sharsted Wood in a straight line for 800m to Sharsted Court. Here, bend round to the right, head along the right-hand of a pair of driveways and then descend the steep lane beyond back down into Newnham. A final left turn takes you past Calico House back to the start.

35

Leysdown-on-Sea and the Isle of Harty

Distance 10.5km **Time** 2 hours 45
Terrain paths and tracks along sea walls
and over marshland **Map** OS Explorer 149
Access bus to Leysdown from Sheerness
and Sittingbourne

**A foray across the marshland of the far
southeast corner of the Isle of Sheppey
brings you to Kent's remotest church.**

  The walk starts from Leysdown's coastal
car park on the Isle of Sheppey at
Neptune's Beach, 1.5km south of the
centre of Leysdown-on-Sea along
Shellness Road. There are also some
spaces for cars alongside Shellness Road
itself, north of Neptune's Beach. The Isle
of Sheppey lies off the North Kent coast
and is surrounded by the tidal waters of
the Thames Estuary and The Swale.
People used to refer to the place as the
Isles of Sheppey, with the southwest part

still called Elmley Island and the remoter
southeast corner, the Isle of Harty.
  Leysdown is a popular seaside resort
and it can become very busy. The area has
a historical association with early
attempts at flying aeroplanes and the
Wright Brothers even visited Leysdown in
1909 to inspect the planes being
constructed there. The route also passes
through Swale National Nature Reserve,
which gives a real sense of remoteness
and is a haven in winter for birds such as
oystercatchers, knot, dunlin and grey
and golden plover, as well as breeding
lapwings and redshank in spring.
  From the car park, climb the bank up
onto the sea wall and turn right for 1.5km
towards the hamlet of Shellness. A little
before the hamlet you pass Swale Naturist
Beach – there is a 20m buffer zone in place
alongside the beach on the left and the

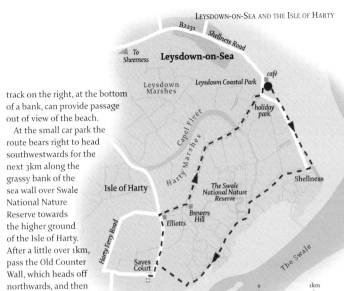

track on the right, at the bottom of a bank, can provide passage out of view of the beach.

At the small car park the route bears right to head southwestwards for the next 3km along the grassy bank of the sea wall over Swale National Nature Reserve to the higher ground of the Isle of Harty. After a little over 1km, pass the Old Counter Wall, which heads off northwards, and then dogleg left and right to continue alongside a channel. About halfway along this section there is a viewing hide. Keep on past the hide, with saltmarsh to the left and former saltworks on the right, to a gate where the sea wall bends right.

Continue diagonally over the field beyond to a gate and sign for Harty Church, beyond which a track takes you inland for 600m up to a track junction. It is worth a detour left for 300m to Harty Church, which, despite being known as the remotest church in Kent, still attracts visitors and pilgrims. From the track junction, the onward route heads northwards for just under 1km up the track past Forge Cottage and through the farm buildings at Elliotts, before turning right past Elliotts Farmhouse

and along the concrete track to Brewers Hill Farmhouse.

Carry on along the track, which now bends to the left, up between fields and over a slight rise. After just over 1km the track bends to the right and heads alongside a ditch past where the Old Counter Wall comes in from the right. Beyond this point a narrower path continues ahead for 100m to a gate and track junction. Bear left up the track for 500m to the next gate by a barn, beyond which you pass the garden entrance to Muswell Manor and then turn right to reach Shellness Road. Here, a left turn along the road will take you back to the start.

◀ The North Kent coast from Leysdown Coastal Park

37

Faversham and Ham Marshes

Distance 8.5km **Time** 2 hours
Terrain creekside paths and saltmarsh
fields, muddy if wet **Map** OS Explorer 149
Access bus to Faversham from
Canterbury, Maidstone and Ashford;
train to Faversham from London,
Chatham, Canterbury and Dover

**There's plenty of history and wildlife to
see on this walk from one of Kent's most
important ports.**

Faversham is in origin a port and
medieval market town with a long history.
Its name combines the Roman word for
'smith' or 'craftsman', *faber*, and the Saxon
ham, meaning 'homestead'. The town was
part of the Confederation of Cinque Ports
and was ideally situated for trade on a
tidal creek with access to The Swale and
Thames Estuary. Today, the town contains
hundreds of listed buildings and it is
well worth wandering around the old
streets, squares and quays. One industry

which still survives is the Shepherd
Neame Brewery, Britain's oldest brewer,
and the weekly and monthly Charter
Market in the town, dating from at least
the 11th century, is claimed to be the
oldest in Kent.

From the Market Place in the centre of
Faversham by the Guildhall, head down
West Street past shops and houses to
North Lane. Turn right past Shepherd
Neame Brewery and then left along Bridge
Road over Faversham Creek.

Here, a right turn takes you along Front
Brents on the Saxon Shore Way beside
Faversham Creek. After passing the area
known as Crab Island on the left, the
Saxon Shore Way detours away from the
creek around Faversham Reach housing
development, the former site of Pollocks'
shipyard. At its entrance, dogleg briefly
left, then right to stay on the Saxon Shore
Way and pass into marshy fields before
bending back right to the creek.

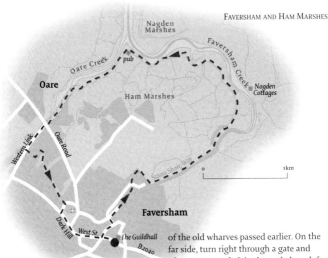

of the old wharves passed earlier. On the far side, turn right through a gate and after 100m, at a fork in the path, keep left between houses and alongside a hedge up to the junction with Priory Road.

Here, a right turn takes you to the junction with Dark Hill, where you turn left down the pavement to Stonebridge Pond at the bottom, now a place for feeding the ducks but once at the heart of the gunpowder industry in the town. Chart Mills, located a short detour off to the right along Westbrook Walk, is a surviving part of four groups of mills, which used waterpower for the manufacture of gunpowder. Faversham, owing to its access to the sea, was one of the most important centres of gunpowder production until the end of the 19th century, when high explosives replaced gunpowder, and the works finally closed in 1934. For the final part of the walk, keep ahead along West Street, over North Lane, and back up to the Market Place.

You now turn left and continue on the raised bank alongside the creek, past Standard Quay on the opposite bank, out onto Ham Marshes. After 1km the Saxon Shore Way bends left away from the creek and winds its way northwards and westwards over the saltmarsh to The Shipwrights Arms at the confluence with Oare Creek. Here, turn left past moorings and a marina before heading a little away from Oare Creek to reach a lane. Bear right along the lane and beside the creek to the crossroads on the edge of Oare.

Head over the crossroads and along the pavement of the B2045 for just under 300m, where a footpath forks off left by a bus stop. The footpath runs parallel with the road and then zigzags its way between tall fencing around a large distribution centre – the modern equivalent perhaps

◀ Faversham Creek near Hollowshore

Selling and Perry Wood

Distance 5km **Time** 1 hour 30
Terrain orchards, woodland and lanes
Map OS Explorer 149 **Access** train from
Chatham and Canterbury to Selling
Station, 1.5km to the northeast of Selling
over fields and orchards

**This undulating route ambles through
delightful orchards and woods to a
long-established viewing point.**

Perry Wood is classed as ancient
woodland and lies in a landscape of low
hills surrounded by fields and orchards.
The viewpoint of The Pulpit is the main
attraction at the southern end of the
wood and it is thought to have been given
this name from the practice of preaching
sermons from the spot. The route also
passes through an area, now a car park,
known as The Bandstand, so-called
because of the Salvation Army bands that
used to play here in Victorian times and
where there was even the custom of

serving afternoon teas. Alas, the cakes,
crumpets and scones are no more. The
area is also designated as a Local Wildlife
Site and is a haven for woodland flowers,
insects, fungi and some rare hybrid trees.
There are also reports of dormice
breeding, for whom the abundance of
coppice stools and leaf litter are essential
for hibernating in winter.

The walk starts from the village of
Selling, where there is a car park on its
western edge near the school. Walk up
through the centre of the village past the
White Lion pub and, just before Selling
Court road, turn right onto a footpath.
Head up past houses and then up a small
field with an orchard on its right to the
top of the rise. The footpath now bears a
little right and passes through the
orchard beyond. On its far side, a quick
dogleg right, then left across a track takes
you up the right-hand edge of the next
orchard, at the end of which the footpath

◀ Traditional cottage in Perry Wood

passes through the hedge and over a stile into the field beyond. Head over the field, past a house called Puddledock and down its driveway to a lane.

Cross the lane and, a little to the right, continue ahead on the bridleway up into Perry Wood. The bridleway rises gently over the shoulder of the hill through the woodland to the lane by the Rose and Crown pub. Head past the pub and up a track to a house. Here, the bridleway passes to the right of the house and its garden to a bridleway junction. Turn left steeply uphill and, at the top of the rise, bear right for 250m to The Mount, with its viewpoint called The Pulpit, which has boards carved with local topographical features.

Continue past The Pulpit down some broad steps to the bridleway junction and turn left. In 75m, at the next junction, fork left with the bridleway which bends left and heads northwards for the next 600m up through Conduit Wood on a winding and undulating path, before bending left to reach a five-way track and path junction by the driveway to a house. Here, bear right down across a footbridge and, just beyond, fork right past a stand of young chestnut trees, steeply up over the rise and down to a lane, across which is Perry Wood car park and picnic site, known as The Bandstand.

Cross the car park and continue along the bridleway, which leads gently down past a house and garden to a lane. Keep

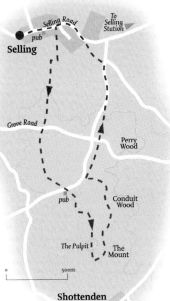

on down the narrow lane past Downwell Cottage and Downwell House for 300m to the junction. Here, take the footpath which heads off left along a track and past an orchard. In just under 100m you'll need to bear a little to the right, over a farm lane and alongside the orchard beyond to reach Selling Road. From here, turn left up the road and round the left-hand bend (where the footpath from Selling Station comes in) back into the centre of Selling.

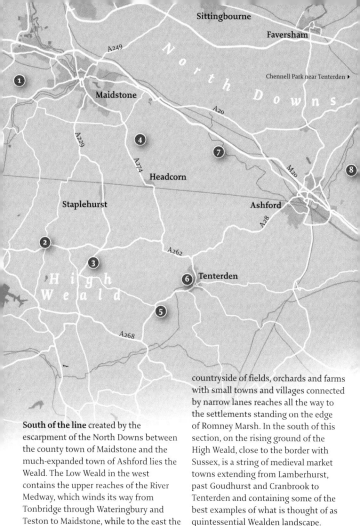

Sittingbourne

Faversham

A249

North Downs

Chennell Park near Tenterden ▶

Maidstone

A20

A229

A274

4

7

Headcorn

Staplehurst

Ashford

A28

2

A262

3

High
Weald

6

Tenterden

5

A268

8

M20

South of the line created by the escarpment of the North Downs between the county town of Maidstone and the much-expanded town of Ashford lies the Weald. The Low Weald in the west contains the upper reaches of the River Medway, which winds its way from Tonbridge through Wateringbury and Teston to Maidstone, while to the east the

countryside of fields, orchards and farms with small towns and villages connected by narrow lanes reaches all the way to the settlements standing on the edge of Romney Marsh. In the south of this section, on the rising ground of the High Weald, close to the border with Sussex, is a string of medieval market towns extending from Lamberhurst, past Goudhurst and Cranbrook to Tenterden and containing some of the best examples of what is thought of as quintessential Wealden landscape.

Maidstone, Ashford and the Weald

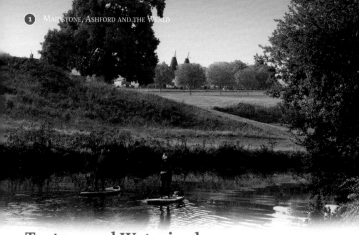

Teston and Wateringbury

Distance 5km **Time** 1 hour 15
Terrain riverside paths and fields, liable
to flooding **Map** OS Explorer 148
Access bus to Teston from Maidstone,
Tonbridge and Tunbridge Wells stops on
the A26 (opposite The Street), 400m from
the start; train to Wateringbury, halfway
along the route, from Maidstone West
and Tonbridge

**The peaceful banks and meadows of the
River Medway set the scene for a simple
circuit from Teston Bridge Country Park.**

The walk starts from Teston Bridge
Country Park, where there is a car park,
toilets and a snack kiosk. Teston
(pronounced Teeson) is situated just off
the A26, about 5km to the west of
Maidstone. The country park takes its
name from the bridge that spans the River
Medway here. In origin the bridge dates
from the 15th century, though its arches

were rebuilt several times to improve
navigation on the river in the 19th century
and the whole structure was restored
more recently in the 1970s. There are
riverside meadows and natural wetland
habitats which provide a haven for birds
and mammals. On Bridge Meadow, just by
the car park, there is also a large grassy
area suitable for picnics. Dogs under close
control are welcome in the park.

From the car park cross Bridge Meadow
towards the River Medway and turn right
onto the towing path, which heads over a
footbridge to Teston Lock. The riverside
path continues through a gate into
Coombe Hill meadow, where Shetland
cattle are kept to help manage the area of
grassland. At the far end of the meadow
the path leaves the country park and
continues beside the river along a grassy
section and through an area of willow and
alder to Hampstead and Yalding Cruising

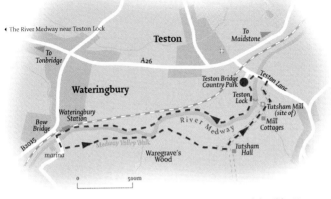

◄ The River Medway near Teston Lock

Club. Keep on past the moorings and along the riverside track past the rear of Wateringbury Station to Bow Bridge Marina and the road at Wateringbury. The station is accessible from here over the far side of the level crossing.

At Wateringbury the route turns left over Bow Bridge and past Medway Wharf Marina on the right, where there is the delightful Ramblers Rest café in one of the old wharf sheds. You now turn left off the road onto the Medway Valley Walk, which passes through the gate to a path junction in the field and then follows the left-hand path straight ahead alongside the fence, with the River Medway away to the left, over three fields to a boardwalk and footbridge into Waregrave's Wood. Continue through the wood, now close to the river, and into fields again, where the Medway Valley Walk bears half-right away from the river up a grassy slope and over a field towards the buildings of Tutsham Hall.

Continue along the driveway past Tutsham Cottage and the Cider House. Before the Hall itself, with its prominent oast chimneys, turn left with the Medway Valley Walk through the gate by the cattle grid and follow the driveway downhill with views over the Medway Valley. Keep on past a Second World War pillbox overlooking the river and continue past Mill Cottages and Mill House to the site of Tutsham Oil Mill. The industrial complex of this former 19th-century linseed oil mill would have presented an imposing sight and the noise of its machinery would have been in stark contrast to the tranquility of the area now.

The final part of the walk continues up the lane beyond the mill, round the left bend and down to the B2163. Here, cross the road, go to the right up some steps and then turn sharp left onto a permissive path leading downhill parallel with the road to Teston Bridge. A little care is needed with any traffic crossing the narrow bridge, before you turn left back into Teston Bridge Country Park.

Goudhurst

Distance 5.5km **Time** 1 hour 30
Terrain lanes and field paths
Map OS Explorer 136 **Access** bus to
Goudhurst from Tunbridge Wells
and Tenterden

**A stroll over undulating countryside from
one of Kent's prettiest villages takes you
through the heart of the Weald.**

Goudhurst is an attractive straggling
village with its Church of St Mary perched
on top of a steep hill. The tower is open to
visitors in the summer months and inside
the church, among the many memorials,
are the rare monument in painted wood
to 'Old' Sir Alexander Culpeper and his
wife, Constance, and the alabaster wall
monument of 'Young' Sir Alexander
Culpeper with his 16 grandchildren.

Stories of smuggling in the region are
plentiful, but the one most often
associated with Goudhurst involves the
notorious Hawkhurst Gang. In the middle
of the 18th century the feared gang were

plying their criminal contraband trade,
but in 1747 the village of Goudhurst,
undeterred by the gang's reputation for
brutality, formed a local militia to bring
them to justice. Thomas Kingsmill, one of
the gang's leaders and a native of the
village, was outraged at such a show of
resistance and threatened to slaughter the
inhabitants and burn down the town.
During the fighting around the church the
villagers killed a number of the gang and
saw off the rest. Kingsmill escaped but
was later arrested, convicted and, in 1749,
hanged at Tyburn. His body was returned
to Goudhurst to be hung up in chains.

Walk down the High Street from
St Mary's Church and turn right down
North Road. Just past the bus stop take
the footpath off left along a footway,
leading steeply down between gardens
and then down three fields to the lane by
Goudhurst water treatment works. Cross
over the lane and continue across the field
beyond to Lidwell Lane. Dogleg right for

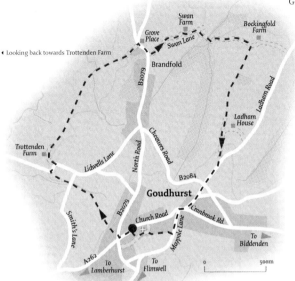

◀ Looking back towards Trottenden Farm

Swan Farm
Bockingfold Farm
Grove Place
Swan Lane
Brandfold
B2079
Ladham Road
Ladham House
Cheveners Road
Trottenden Farm
Lidwells Lane
North Road
B2084
Goudhurst
B2079
Smith's Lane
Church Road
Cranbrook Rd
A262
Maypole Lane
To Biddenden
To Lamberhurst
To Flimwell

0   500m

50m along the lane to the bend, then left onto a footpath down the drive to Trottenden Farm and bear right in front of the farm's oast chimneys. The route now heads over two fields, past a stand of trees and over a staggered crosspaths. Keep on down the right-hand edge of the next field to a footbridge, beyond which the path climbs up through some woodland, past the Pump House and up its drive to the B2079 at Brandfold.

Dogleg right along the verge for 100m to the bend, then left onto the bridleway which leads along Swan Lane. You soon bend right past Swan Cottage to Swan Farm, where the footpath forks right into fields. Head along the edge of the first field, then turn right with the bridleway

down across a stream and up the field on the far side to the entrance to Bockingfold Farm. Turn right and follow the footpath for 1km up a track, which rises steadily between fields and up the driveway of Ladham House to Ladham Road. Continue ahead up Ladham Road, across the B2084 and along the narrow lane opposite to Cranbrook Road, the A262.

Turn right along the pavement to the bend, then cross the road and follow Maypole Lane past the grassy green and down the hill for 100m to Maypole Cottages. Here, take the footpath off right up steps and along the top of a field to Back Lane, once the only highway through the village, which will bring you back to St Mary's Church and the start.

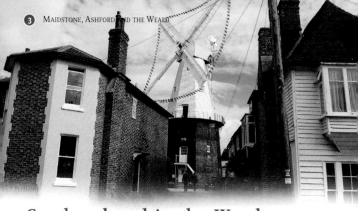

Cranbrook and Angley Wood

**Distance 4.25km Time 1 hour 15
Terrain fields and woodland
Map OS Explorer 136 Access bus to
Cranbrook from Maidstone, Hawkhurst,
Tunbridge Wells and Tenterden**

**This woodland circuit is short enough to
leave plenty of time to explore the
historic town of Cranbrook.**

Cranbrook is another Wealden village
that it pays to spend some time
wandering around and seeing what there
is to discover. The small town draws its
fair share of tourists, not least for the
good number of cafés and teashops. This
walk heads for the woods to the west of
Cranbrook, but it is also worth making
the short walk to the eastern edge of the
town (down Stone Street, over St David's
Bridge and up The Hill) to see the Union
Windmill, England's tallest smock mill. It
was built early in the 19th century and the
reason for its height was to allow its
sweeps to catch the wind above the roofs

of the surrounding houses. In the 1980s
the Cranbrook Windmill Association was
formed and since then it has managed
and operated the mill. The mill is still
working and is open to the public on
some weekday and weekend afternoons
during the summer (unionmill.org.uk).

The town is also well known for its
Church of St Dunstan, the 'Cathedral of
the Weald'. Whilst not a true cathedral, its
size and architecture is impressive, a
result of the wealth of Flemish weavers
who settled in Cranbrook in the 14th
century. Inside, a numbered tour has been
created, with an accompanying leaflet to
help visitors appreciate the monuments
and layout. Particularly striking at the
west end of the nave are the four Green
Men, elaborately carved as medieval oak
shields and originally used as roof-bosses.
Amongst the many other things to see are
a rare total immersion font and a detailed
memorial family tree on the wall of the
side chapel.

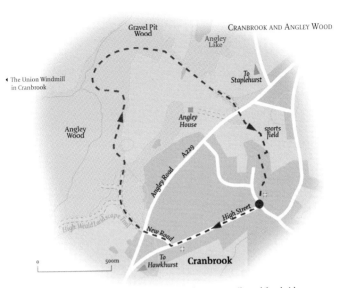

Gravel Pit
Wood

Angley
Lake

To
Staplehurst

◄ The Union Windmill
in Cranbrook

Angley
House

sports
field

Angley
Wood

A229

Angley Road

High Weald Landscape Trail

High Street

New Road

0   500m

To
Hawkhurst   **Cranbrook**

Walk up Cranbrook's long High Street, following the route of the High Weald Landscape Trail, past shops and houses. At the fire station keep on uphill past the Catholic Church of St Theodore and follow the High Weald Landscape Trail off right up New Road and across Angley Road, the A229, into Angley Wood.

Follow the track up round the bend, where the High Weald Landscape Trail forks off left, and continue along the main track to a prominent fork by some Scots pine trees. The route keeps right and, in 150m, heads down to the left before bending back right. At the next fork keep right along a straight level section for 250m and just as the path rises again, at a path junction, turn left and follow a narrower path downhill between banks and round a right-hand bend to a

metal squeeze-stile and footbridge near the bottom edge of the wood, with a stream below in a dell.

Cross the footbridge and, at the path junction a little beyond, fork right down across a second footbridge. From here, the route heads uphill and then alongside a fence up to the top of the wood. Continue ahead along the fence and pass between fields, down across a dip and up to a driveway, which leads in 100m to Angley Cottage and Angley Road. Cross the road and head down a fenced path and straight up the field beyond to a path junction. A right turn takes you alongside playing fields, before a dogleg right, then left past the entrance to Cranbrook CofE Primary School and along a footway to St Dunstan's Church brings you back to the High Street.

Sutton Valence and Ulcombe

Distance 8.5km **Time** 2 hours 15
Terrain lanes, fields and orchards
Map OS Explorer 137 **Access** bus to Sutton
Valence from Maidstone, Headcorn and
Tenterden

**Start on a high along the Greensand
Ridge before rambling back over the
fields and orchards that lie beneath.**

Sutton Valence sits on the escarpment
of the Greensand Ridge overlooking the
Vale of Kent and the Weald. The village
still has the remains of a 12th-century
Norman castle on its eastern edge, which
is accessible off Rectory Lane near the end
of the walk. Today only the stone keep
remains but originally there was an inner
and outer bailey, as well as a barbican, a
fortified gateway and, until the early 20th
century, ruins of a curtain wall and a
second tower. However, by clambering up
the steps to the keep, it is still easy to see
why the location was chosen and from
the panoramic views you can get a sense
of what a commanding position the castle
would have had, close as it is to the road
from Maidstone and dominating the
Weald of Kent.

Walk along the High Street with its
cobbled pavement and old houses, past
Sutton Valence School's arts centre, a
former chapel, and up Broad Street on the
raised footway over Tumblers Hill and
along the lane to the junction with
Pleasure House Lane. Here, fork left off
the lane and follow the Greensand Way
markers along the edge of an orchard for
250m and then left through the orchard
down to Workhouse Lane. The Greensand
Way continues ahead along Church Lane,
past the Church of St Peter and St Paul
and the entrance to East Sutton Park to
Charlton Lane.

Keep ahead onto the bridleway into
fields, down across a dip and up to Morry
Lane. The Greensand Way doglegs left up
the lane to Morry House and then right
along the top of a field and down
alongside an orchard on a wide track to
reach Church Farm and All Saints Church
above the village of Ulcombe. There is
likely to have been a church here since the

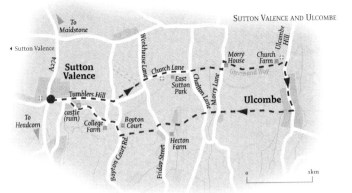

6th century, though the current building originates from the 12th century. Inside are several 13th century wall-paintings, one depicting St Michael and the Devil weighing souls and another the story of Dives (the Rich Man) and Lazarus (the Beggar). At the road beyond, you leave the Greensand Way and turn right down Ulcombe Hill into the village itself. Continue down to the bottom and just before the school turn right onto a footpath which takes you past houses into fields again.

The return route now heads in a westerly direction back along a series of field paths. At the end of the first field, cross the footbridge over a stream, beyond which you head across the bottom corner of an orchard and past a patch of woodland. Now take the track ahead, to the left of a ditch, up between covered strawberry fields, over the rise and down past a lake to Morry Lane. In the field beyond, the path bears a little to the left to a gate and then passes up the side of railings and a playing field on the right to reach Charlton Lane.

Carry on over two more fields, bearing left at the marker post, before heading up between orchards and through Willow Wood to a footbridge on the far side. You now pass over the rise in the field ahead, with East Sutton Park off to the right, and down to Friday Street. Here, a short dogleg left, then right over the lane takes you past the reservoir below Hecton Farm. At the end of this field, bear left through the gap in the hedge and make sure you head uphill on the left-hand side of a ditch and then a hedge to reach Boyton Court Road.

You'll need a bit of stamina for the last part of the walk as you turn right up the steep lane past cottages to the entrance to Boyton Court. Take the bridleway opposite off left to the junction by College Farm and continue ahead along a track, which joins a lane up past houses to a junction. Fork left down Rectory Lane and round the bend to the entrance to Sutton Valence Castle, accessible up steps on the right. Further along Rectory Lane you reach the junction with Chapel Road, where you turn right to the High Street.

Rolvenden and Rolvenden Layne

Distance 6km **Time** 1 hour 30
Terrain fields, lanes **Map** OS Explorer 125
Access bus to Rolvenden from Ashford,
Tenterden and Tunbridge Wells

**If you are after peace and quiet, you'll
appreciate these storybook villages set in
rolling countryside.**

Located southwest of Tenterden is the
small village of Rolvenden and the hamlet
of Rolvenden Layne, which was extended
considerably after a large fire in the 1660s
in Rolvenden left many villagers
homeless. Between the two settlements is
Great Maytham Hall, an old mansion
rebuilt in 1910 in neo-Georgian style by
the architect Sir Edwin Lutyens for its
then owner Harold Tennant. Later
Lutyens also designed the memorial to
the owner's son Henry Tennant, killed
during the First World War in France. This
can be seen in the Church of St Mary,
while nearby stands Rolvenden's war
memorial, likewise completed to a
Lutyens design.

The Hall also has a literary connection

with the English-American novelist and
playwright Frances Hodgson Burnett, who
lived here between 1898 and 1907 and is
perhaps best known as the author of the
popular novel *Little Lord Fauntleroy*. As well
as writing more than 40 novels and plays,
Burnett loved gardening and the rose
garden at Great Maytham Hall is said to
have inspired her later book, *The Secret
Garden*, published in 1909 when she had
moved back to America.

From the southern end of Rolvenden
village at the junction of the A28 with
Maytham Road, take the footpath past the
Church of St Mary to the far side of the
churchyard into fields, where the path
forks. Keep left along the route of the
High Weald Landscape Trail, which is
followed for the outward part of the route.
The trail heads over three fields, down the
first field, then up over the shoulder of
the two fields beyond to a gate into
woodland. Keep on through the woodland
and then past Great Maytham Hall on a
fenced section of path to a gate and
crosspaths on the far side of the wood.

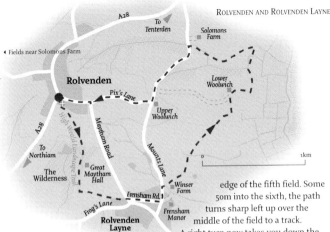

◄ Fields near Solomons Farm

Here, the trail turns left along the edges of two fields and a fenced section to reach the edge of Rolvenden Layne. Cross Maytham Road and head along Frensham Road to the junction with Mounts Lane, opposite the entrance to Frensham Manor. To visit the Ewe and Lamb pub you can detour right off Frensham Road after 200m down a narrow walkway.

A left turn down Mounts Lane takes you to the stream at the bottom. Here, the High Weald Landscape Trail turns right along the drive to the Coach House and then bears left in front of its entrance over a series of six fields to the houses of Lower Woolwich – the waymarks show the way over the first field, down the edge of the second, over a ditch and across the bottom corner of the next field, before heading up over the shoulder to the far side of the fourth; turn right along the field edge for 50m, then dogleg left through the hedge and right down the edge of the fifth field. Some 50m into the sixth, the path turns sharp left up over the middle of the field to a track.

A right turn now takes you down the winding track past the houses of Lower Woolwich into fields again, with a good view ahead across the crayfish lagoons to the high ground of the Quarter, south of Tenterden. A little before the bottom of the first field the trail turns left through the hedge to head up over the shoulder of the field beyond and a little to the left to reach a marker post at the edge of a marshy area. Keep ahead alongside a drainage ditch and over a footbridge to reach a footpath junction in the field beyond, marked by a fingerpost.

Leave the High Weald Landscape Trail here and turn sharp left to a stile, beyond which you follow the right-hand edge up two fields to reach a lane. Turn left uphill along the tree-lined lane for 700m to the houses of Upper Woolwich, where a right turn along Pix's Lane brings you up to its junction with Maytham Road in another 600m. Turn right along the pavement past houses to return to the start.

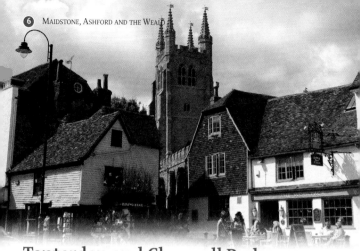

Tenterden and Chennell Park

Distance 3.5km **Time** 1 hour
Terrain fields and parkland
Map OS Explorer 125 **Access** bus to
Tenterden from Ashford, Maidstone
and Tunbridge Wells

**A short foray over fields and parkland
sets off from one of Kent's finest towns.**

Tenterden's mix of architectural styles
gives it a picture-postcard look. Victorian
houses and Georgian buildings share the
streets with traditional Kent tile-knapped
and weather-boarded frontages. The town
is sometimes referred to as the 'Jewel of
the Weald' and it certainly draws its fair
share of visitors, not least for its
tearooms, cafés, pubs and shops or to ride
on the East Sussex and Kent Railway.

There are quite a few theories about the
origins of the town's name. The most
popular is that this area of the Weald was
known as *Tenet wara denn*, 'the den of the
Thanet folk', and this certainly ties in
with the dedication of the town's church
to St Mildred, who lived in Kent in the
8th century and was Abbess of Thanet.
Another is that the name records a
Thane's appointment of a Warden to
administer the town, by which its name,
through a variety of spellings, became
Tenterden. Others point to a connection
with wooden tenters, the wooden frames
used in cloth manufacture, and the *denn*,
or *dene*, meaning 'forest clearing'. More
certain is the town's history of cloth
manufacture, which ensured it was part
of the Confederacy of the Cinque Ports
and annexed to the town and port of
Rye. The Woolpack Inn still stands on the
High Street near the churchyard, and has
done so since the 16th century. The walk
begins from here.

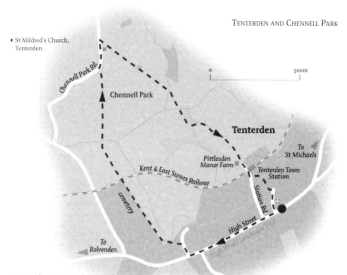

◄ St Mildred's Church,
Tenterden

Chennell Park Rd.

▲ Chennell Park

0   500m

Tenterden

To
St Michaels

Pittlesden
Manor Farm

Kent & East Sussex Railway

Tenterden Town
Station

cemetery

Station Rd.

High Street

High Weald Landscape Trail

To
Rolvenden

From the centre of Tenterden walk along the broad High Street past shops and cafés to the west end of the town. A little past the junction with the B2082 to Rye, turn right along Westwell Court and in 50m, just before the bend, take the footpath off left into fields. The footpath heads down a long narrow field and bends to the right past the upper entrance to the cemetery. In another 50m bear left through a gate into the cemetery and follow the path down its right-hand edge. At the bottom keep ahead and cross the Kent and East Sussex Railway line, beyond which you descend three more fields to a footbridge over a stream in Chennell Park.

The route continues across the footbridge and over the field beyond, then heads up over the parkland along a fenced path to a lane. Follow the lane for just over 100m to a crosspaths by the gates to a house, then turn right to leave it. The footpath leads alongside a high garden wall and between park paling before descending through the parkland, with a good view across the valley to the tower of St Mildred's Church. At the bottom cross two footbridges and climb the field beyond, where the path forks. Make sure you stick to the left-hand field edge to reach the five-bar gate in the corner.

Here, bear left into the trees and follow the banked path uphill and around to the right, up along the backs of houses to the car park of the Kent and East Sussex Railway. Head up through the car park, past the entrance to Tenterden Town Station and over the level crossing. Just beyond this, turn left up Church Path for a final short climb up to St Mildred's Church and the High Street.

55

Egerton and Pluckley

Distance 11km **Time** 3 hours
Terrain old lanes, fields and orchards
Map OS Explorer 137 **Access** bus to
Egerton, Pluckley and Little Chart from
Ashford (limited service)

**An undulating and well-waymarked
route wanders between three secluded
villages in the heart of orchard country.**

The villages of Egerton, Pluckley and
Little Chart lie down narrow lanes to the
west of Ashford. Two ancient families, the
Darrells and the Derings, are connected
with these villages. In St James' Church in
Egerton are the impressive Darrell
Monuments, brought here from the old
St Mary's, Little Chart. Closely associated
with Pluckley is the Dering family of
Surrenden. One of the most interesting
members was Sir Edward Dering who gave
his name to *The Dering Manuscript*, the
earliest manuscript of Shakespeare's to
survive. In the Civil War he also escaped
the Roundheads by fleeing out of an arch-
topped window. In recognition of this it
was later decided that all buildings on the
estate should have arch-topped windows.

From the centre of Egerton, walk down
Rock Hill Road and, opposite the primary
school, follow the Greensand Way off left,
down past houses and along a path
between fields up to Stone Hill Road.
Dogleg right for 100m, then left along the
drive of Stone Hill Farm to a gate before
descending a track into fields. Walk along
the top of two fields to Greenhill Lane.
Here, turn right to the bend and, by
Greenhill House, carry straight on into
fields. Head down across a stream and
then bear right down the edge of four
fields to a track. Dogleg right, then left

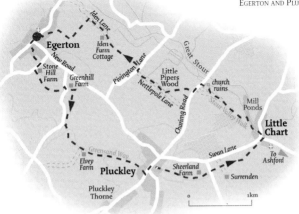

over two more fields to Elvey Farm. The Greensand Way leads past the buildings and then up over five more fields to Pluckley. At the road turn left up Forge Hill, past the turn for the village centre.

Keep on up the hill for another 50m and turn right alongside the sports field. Continue to follow the Greensand Way beside a series of orchards, past Sheerland Farm, through more orchards and over a lane. You now pass along a garden wall and then the edges of two fields before emerging into orchards again, with the house of Surrenden off to the right. In the second orchard, after 50m at a marker post, fork left down through plum trees and along a grassy track to Little Chart.

The route now leaves the Greensand Way and turns left past the Swan Inn and the turn for the village centre. Follow the Stour Valley Walk ahead into fields. At the end of the first field go around the corner for 50m and turn right up a track between fields, over the rise and down past farm buildings to the ruins of St Mary's Church, destroyed by a flying bomb in 1944. Continue through the churchyard to the road. The Stour Valley Walk doglegs left for 150m up the road past the entrance to Chart Court, then right over two fields and through Little Pipers Wood to a byway.

Turn right along the byway, dogleg over Pivington Lane, and continue for 250m to a path junction. The Stour Valley Walk turns off right downhill, but the onward route carries on along the byway past Iden Farm Cottage and then along Iden Lane for another 400m. Just past a house called Iden, turn left onto a footpath up past a cottage and along the field beyond. At the end of the field turn right along a tree-lined path for 200m, where a footpath heads off left up the field towards Egerton Church and over two paddocks to houses. Follow the right of way along a walkway, through a garden gate and along the left-hand edge of a garden, before turning right for the centre of the village.

◄ On the final approach to Egerton

Wye Downs

**Distance 7km Time 2 hours
Terrain fields and downs, with one steep
descent Map OS Explorer 137 Access bus
to Wye from Ashford and Canterbury;
train from Ashford and Canterbury to
Wye Station, 700m from the start along
the North Downs Way**

**Climb onto the North Downs for some of
the most impressive views from the
famous Wye Crown.**

The small town of Wye lies below the
escarpment of the North Downs and
stands on the Great Stour, where it cuts
through the downs between Ashford and
Canterbury. On the slope to the north of
the town, above an old chalk pit, a crown
was cut in 1902 to mark the coronation of
Edward VII. At the time the principal of
Wye College thought that his agricultural
college students would be put to good
use digging out the chalk and removing
the barrowloads of spoil to the nearby

chalk pit. The students were also used to
create the outline of the crown. A paper
cut-out of a crown was stuck onto the
lens of a theodolite and then the
students, carrying flags on poles, were
directed into position until the correct
line had been traced on the ground.
A little further along the escarpment from
the Wye Crown is Wye National Nature
Reserve, which encloses the Devil's
Kneading Trough, one of a number of
steep-sided coombes on the downs,
created at the end of the last ice age as
torrents of melted snow and ice flowed
down the slopes. Both vantage points
are passed along the route and give
outstanding views southwards.

The walk starts in the village of Wye at
the top of Church Street by the Church
of St Gregory and St Martin. Follow the
North Downs Way across the churchyard
to the right of the church, past
allotments, and turn right to Olantigh

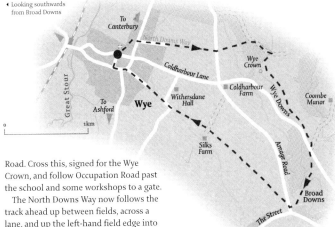

◄ Looking southwards from Broad Downs

Road. Cross this, signed for the Wye Crown, and follow Occupation Road past the school and some workshops to a gate.

The North Downs Way now follows the track ahead up between fields, across a lane, and up the left-hand field edge into woodland, with the Wye Crown just visible through the trees up on the right. The path leads steeply up through the trees; where the gradient eases, keep left at a fork in the path to reach a lane.

Turn right up the wooded lane for 250m and, where the trees end, follow the North Downs Way as it turns right up steps to the top of the Wye Downs escarpment. The Way now turns left along the top of the escarpment for just over 1km, passing above the Wye Crown and its viewpoint to a gate, and then alongside the fence and down to the drive to Coombe Manor. Here, turn right to Coldharbour Lane.

Cross the lane and continue along the North Downs Way which forks left for the Devil's Kneading Trough. At the third gate the route leaves the North Downs Way and turns right to drop down the steep west side of the coombe. The path descends the grassy slope above the

Devil's Kneading Trough, down past a topograph and bench, with long views over Romney Marsh and the downs near Hastings. Continue down the steep slope to a gate and then keep left down to a second gate onto Amage Road.

A dogleg right for 30m, then left through the hedge takes you into fields for the return along the bottom of the escarpment. Head diagonally across the first field, along the left-hand edge of the second and, in the third field, switch to the other side of the hedge to reach the drive to Silks Farm. Continue ahead in the same direction for the final 1.3 km, past the entrance to Withersdane Hall and then between sports pitches and a field, before heading along Cherry Garden Lane between houses back into Wye. Here, a left turn along Bridge Street will take you to the bottom of Church Street.

59

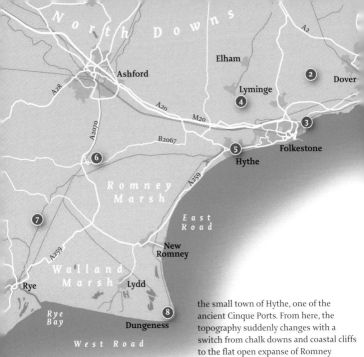

Dover with its port, castle and white cliffs is one of the most visited parts of the county. To the west, between Hawkinge and Alkham, lies one of the prettiest valleys in Kent, while the village of Lyminge and the farming country of the Elham Valley are situated on the southern fringe of the North Downs. Along the coast beyond St Margaret's Bay and South Foreland Lighthouse, which still keeps a lookout over the Goodwin Sands, is the Victorian coastal resort of Folkestone and

the small town of Hythe, one of the ancient Cinque Ports. From here, the topography suddenly changes with a switch from chalk downs and coastal cliffs to the flat open expanse of Romney Marsh. Along the road to Hamstreet and Tenterden, and bordered by the Royal Military Canal, are the villages that fringe the reclaimed land of Romney Marsh and Walland Marsh. Along the coast Dymchurch and St Mary's Bay still host funfairs, amusement arcades and candy-floss sellers next to their sandy beaches and caravan parks, while at the limits of the marsh are found the shingle headland of Dungeness, with its nuclear power station and wildlife reserve, and the Isle of Oxney beyond Appledore, close to the border with Sussex.

St Margaret's Bay and Ness Point ▶

Dover, Folkestone and Romney Marsh

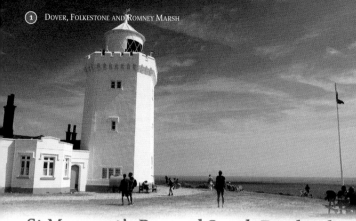

St Margaret's Bay and South Foreland

Distance 7.5km Time 2 hours
Terrain fields, tracks and clifftop paths
Map OS Explorer 138 Access bus to
St Margaret's at Cliffe from Dover,
Deal and Sandwich

This walk passes the Dover Patrol
Monument and along the top of some
of Kent's famous white cliffs to South
Foreland Lighthouse with views out
over the Straits of Dover.

The walk starts from the village of
St Margaret's at Cliffe, where there is
a car park off the High Street near
St Margaret's Church. The church's west
door has some Norman carvings and
inside are Norman pillars and a stained-
glass window memorial to the *Herald of
Free Enterprise* ferry disaster of 1987, in
which three people from the village died.
The route passes the Dover Patrol
Monument, which commemorates those
who lost their lives defending the straits

in the First World War, and also South
Foreland Lighthouse, which overlooks
one of the busiest sea-lanes in the world
and still guards the Goodwin Sands, the
notorious 'ship-swallower'.

Walk along the High Street and turn
right into Kingsdown Road. After 450m
the road becomes a tarmac bridleway
carrying the National Route 1 cyclepath
across Free Down. As the name suggests
this is a former commons, which has been
open land for at least 4000 years. After
650m you pass Little Banks and in another
200m, where the bridleway bends left
downhill, the route leaves the cyclepath
and bears right onto a footpath, through
a gate onto the National Trust land of
Bockhill Farm, with the top of East Hill
and Barrow Mount ahead.

The route now forks sharp right up
between fields and down across the dip
ahead, with views to the obelisk of the
Dover Patrol Monument and the Goodwin

East Hill

Barrow Mount

St Margaret's Free Down

Little Banks

Bockhill Farm

memorial

Free Down

The Leas

Kingsdown Road

Coney Burrow Point

St Margaret's at Cliffe

Sea Street

St Margaret's Bay

Bay Hill

Ness Point

To Dover

Pines Garden

Lighthouse Road

0   1km

Wanstone Farm

Cliff House

lighthouse

◀ South Foreland Lighthouse

Sands. On the far side of the valley the track veers left, then back right, to a bend near agricultural buildings. Here, fork left up the field edge over St Margaret's Free Down to the gate by the Dover Patrol Monument. The monument is an imposing presence and in good weather France is clearly visible – there are similar obelisks at Cap Blanc Nez near Boulogne and also in New York Harbour.

Opposite the obelisk go through the gate onto The Leas and bear right along the clifftop. The path soon descends and then heads more steeply past clifftop houses down to a gate. About 75m beyond, at a marker post, fork left and descend steps to St Margaret's Bay, where a right turn takes you through the seafront car park.

At the far end of the car park continue up the lane past The Coastguard pub to the right-hand bend. Here, fork left with the Saxon Shore Way and then left again past the entrance to the Pines Garden. Continue uphill past houses for another 250m to a five-way track junction and turn left with the Saxon Shore Way up to the bend and through the gate onto

Lighthouse Down. Bear right and follow the clifftop path uphill. After 600m, fork right and rejoin the track up past Cliff House and over the rise, beyond which a left turn with the Saxon Shore Way takes you up to a path junction in front of South Foreland Lighthouse, accessible along its entrance path.

From the junction turn right onto the footpath down between a field and a wood. At the end of the trees turn right along a restricted byway past an area of Access Land and into Lighthouse Road. Continue past houses for another 500m to the road junction at Bay Hill. Here, turn left along the pavement down across the dip and back up into St Margaret's at Cliffe.

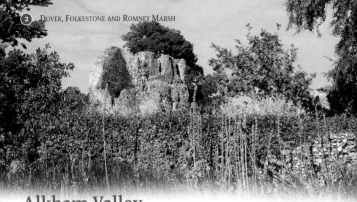

Alkham Valley

Distance 7.5km **Time** 2 hours
Terrain lanes, fields and woodland
Map OS Explorer 138 **Access** bus to
Alkham from Folkestone and Dover

A round of the steep-sided and secluded Alkham Valley takes you past the ruins of a 12th-century abbey.

The walk starts from the village of Alkham, where there is a parking area off Alkham Valley Road, down Hogbrook Hill Lane below the playing field opposite the village hall. The route climbs the steep northern slope of the valley before crossing to its southern side and passing the ruins of St Radegund's Abbey. Since the Dissolution of the Monasteries, the abbey has been in private hands and a working farm. The abbey had been founded in the 12th century by monks from Picardy in northern France. These 'white canons' followed a particularly ascetic life of abstinence, fasting, prayer and care of the sick.

Radegund herself lived in the 6th century and was the daughter of a pagan king of Thuringia. When the Franks invaded she was married off, aged ten, to a Christian king, as his fifth wife. Radegund followed a life of extreme piety and during Lent she even wore a hair-shirt with iron chains and hot plates of iron under her robes. After her brother was murdered by her husband, she fled from court and sought refuge with the Bishop of Noyon. She became a deaconess and later founded the monastery of the Holy Cross at Poitiers.

From the top of Hogbrook Hill Lane by the bus stop walk up Alkham Valley Road past the playing field to the first bend and take the unnamed lane off left past Little Garth and steeply up to the top. Here, pass to the right of a house onto a bridleway up to a field gate, before climbing the field beyond and heading up a hedged section to the top of the hill. The bridleway now turns right by a house and becomes a track, passing between fields and then along a lane past Fryers Ferne

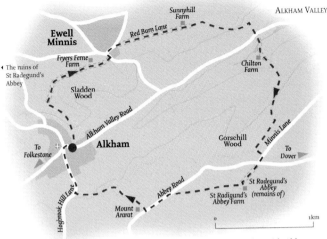

Farm to the road junction in Ewell Minnis.

Here, the route doglegs left to a small green and then right along Newcastle Lane. After 100m fork right along Red Barn Lane to the buildings of Sunnyhill Farm, beyond which the lane becomes a byway through woodland. After 150m, at a path junction, fork right to stay on the byway, down through a patch of woodland, around a right-hand bend and along a section of permissive track down to the valley road.

Head across the road, down the byway opposite to Chilton Farm, up past the farm buildings and along a fenced section up to Gorsehill Wood. The path, now a bridleway, rises steeply up through the trees before levelling out and bending to the right along the top edge of the wood. Where the field on the left ends, keep ahead through woodland again for 150m, before turning left in front of a gate and along to Minnis Lane. Here, a right turn

takes you to the junction with Abbey Road and the entrance to St Radigund's Abbey Farm.

Take the footpath opposite which leads up the farm's driveway and curves left past the ruins of St Radegund's Abbey. The remains are impressive and still act as a gateway to the farmhouse built within the walls. Around the bend a fingerpost marks the way off right over the field for 100m and through a gap in the hedge, where the path splits. Follow the left fork across the large field for 600m to reach Abbey Road again and turn left along the road for 300m to a house called Mount Ararat, where a restricted byway heads off to the right.

Follow the byway, which leads past some stables, dropping gently down through woodland. After 300m, it bends left down to Hogbrook Hill Lane. Here, a right turn down the lane soon brings you back to the parking area and the start.

Folkestone East Cliff and The Warren

Distance 7km **Time** 2 hours 15
Terrain paths at base and on top of cliffs
with sheer drops, one section of steep
ascent **Map** OS Explorer 138 **Access** bus
from Folkestone Bus and Central Railway
Station stops at the north and west end
of Wear Bay Road, 500m from the route

**An adventurous little outing skirts along
the undulating undercliff east of the
Victorian seaside town of Folkestone.**

The Warren, to the east of Folkestone, is
easily missed but the cliffs here, though
perhaps not as famous as their cousins
along the coast at Dover, are no less
dramatic. The undercliff has been subject
to repeated landslip and the process has
created a higgledy-piggledy, semi-wild
shelf of chalk grassland and woodland
between the cliffs and the sea, now

protected as a Site of Special Scientific
Interest. It may come as something of a
surprise to see that the railway line takes
this dramatic route, but its presence has,
at the very least, guaranteed the absence
of other development. When the tide is
out you can access the shore and it's a
great place for some rockpooling. On the
return leg along the top of the cliffs the
route passes the Battle of Britain
Memorial, where there are a number of
monuments and 'The Wing', a visitor
centre with a café overlooking what was
known as Hellfire Corner.

The walk starts on Wear Bay Road at
East Cliff Pavilion car park by the lower of
two Napoleonic-era Martello towers. Head
up the grassy clifftop slope parallel to
Wear Bay Road, where you pass by the site
of a Roman villa, to the upper Martello
tower. Continue up the lane which bends
around the tower, and descend into The
Warren and then alongside the railway to
a fork. Bear right downhill past The
Warren campsite and through a gate to
the track junction by the beach.

QUEEN MOTHER

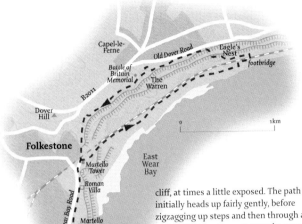

The route forks left a little inland up the clifftop track for the next 1.2km, passing alongside the railway and over a rise, before descending towards the shore again. About 50m before reaching the beach, and just before a metal barrier, look out for a footpath off left. The narrow path heads up steps inland before swinging to the right, parallel with the railway for 100m, to reach a footbridge.

Cross the footbridge over the railway and turn left onto an undulating chalky path, which brings you parallel to the track again for 200m before bearing right into woodland. After 200m you reach a fork, where you keep right and need to ready yourself for the steep climb up the cliff, at times a little exposed. The path initially heads up fairly gently, before zigzagging up steps and then through a series of tighter turns up past the grotto of the Eagle's Nest. A head for heights is useful for the final section of path, which is lined with a wooden balustrade and brings you out onto the top of the cliff and some long views over East Wear Bay.

The route now follows the waymarked England Coast Path and North Downs Way back along the cliffs past the ends of gardens, with some sheer drops in places, before wriggling inland around and across the dip of Steady Hole. Beyond, you reach the lawns of the Battle of Britain Memorial, where you can detour to the right to visit the monuments and visitor centre. The remainder of the route keeps along the clifftop path for another 400m to a footpath junction. Here, turn left with the England Coast Path and descend the East Cliff's ridge back down to the upper Martello tower and the grassy slope beyond back down to the start.

◀ The central statue at the Battle of Britain Memorial, carved by sculptor Harry Gray

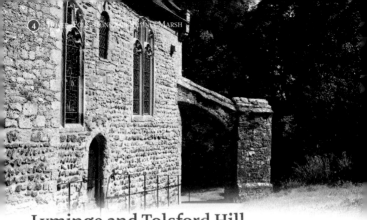

Lyminge and Tolsford Hill

Distance 9km **Time** 2 hours 30
Terrain fields, lanes, one steep climb
Map OS Explorer 138 **Access** bus to
Lyminge from Canterbury and Hythe

A round of the tranquil Elham Valley takes you up and over one of the highest hills in this part of Kent.

Lyminge lies in the Elham Valley and has a rich archaeological record. The church is one of the oldest in Kent and dates from Saxon times. St Ethelburga, daughter of the first Christian king of Kent, is thought to have been buried here, though her tomb is empty. There is a link with St Eadburg, whose sacred well is on the village green, now covered by a Victorian pumphouse. Excavations on the village green have also revealed the foundations of an Anglo-Saxon feasting hall and evidence of people living here as far back as 8000 years ago.

From the High Street in Lyminge head up Church Road, passing the Church of St Mary and St Ethelburga, and bend left down to Mayfield Road, where you can find St Eadburg's Well across the road on the left. Turn right to the bend and then right again up Rectory Lane onto the Elham Valley Way, which is followed for the first half of the walk. At the end of the lane keep on over the fields beyond to Broadstreet Cottage. Cross the road and turn right along the edge of the golf course. After 100m turn left and head between fairways on the left-hand side of a line of trees. At the end of the fairway veer left to a stile onto a road, where a little care is needed.

Across the road the Elham Valley Way heads up three fields towards Tolsford Hill. At the footpath junction just before the communications tower bear right, off the Elham Valley Way, past the tower to the top of the hill for views out to Dungeness and Romney Marsh. The 70m-high tower is constructed of reinforced concrete and was built in 1970 to provide

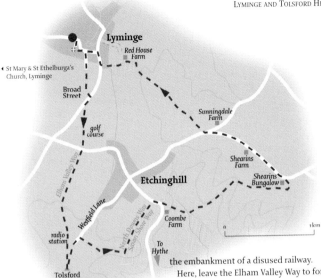

◀ St Mary & St Ethelburga's Church, Lyminge

Lyminge
Red House Farm
Broad Street
golf course
Sunningdale Farm
Shearins Farm
Shearins Bungalow
Etchinghill
Westfield Lane
Coombe Farm
radio station
To Hythe
Tolsford Hill

0   1km

additional phone and television connections to the continent.

To return to the Elham Valley Way, head back on the other side of the tower and turn right into fields just before a gate. Now also on the North Downs Way and Saxon Shore Way, head across the field and through a copse with a view to Summerhouse Hill, before turning left through a gate. Follow the path just inside The Beeches down through the trees and along a field edge to the road. A short dogleg right along the road and then left takes you down to the entrance to Coombe Farm. Turn left over a stile here and head diagonally down the field beyond, through some marshy woodland and over a stream to a path junction by the embankment of a disused railway.

Here, leave the Elham Valley Way to fork left with the North Downs Way, under the railway and up the coombe ahead. Near the top of the steep coombe, bear right to a stile and continue over fields. In the third field, bend left with the fence to an old lane. Here, you leave the North Downs Way and turn left for 100m along the old lane to the junction. The lane, now surfaced, continues gently ahead up past Shearins Farm. Just past the turning to Shuttlesfield take the byway off right. This heads between the golf course and fields and, after 500m, starts its descent down a steeper section past the entrance to Red House Farm. Beyond, follow the tarmac lane down over the disused railway to Station Road. Turn right along the pavement for 100m and then left up Mayfield Road to return to the start.

69

Hythe town and seafront

Distance 4.5km **Time** 1 hour
Terrain town, canal and seafront paths
Map OS Explorer 138 **Access** buses to
Hythe from Folkestone, Ashford
and Canterbury

**Explore one of the original Cinque Ports
on a short but varied stroll.**

Hythe is a coastal town and has a long
association with the sea. It was one of the
original Cinque Ports, established in the
13th century by Royal Charter to protect
the English coastline of Kent and Sussex.
By the 16th century the town's port had
all but silted up and the land between the
town centre and the seafront is now
largely residential. The long High Street
is a delight to wander down and still
contains many historic buildings, as well
as a good number of cafés and teashops.
The Church of St Leonard stands a little
above the High Street and is famous for

its crypt, which contains a medieval
ossuary of more than 1000 human skulls.

In Napoleonic times the threat of
invasion saw the building of the Royal
Military Canal, which stretches 45km from
Seabrook, just to the east of the town, to
Hastings in Sussex, and a series of
Martello towers along the coast. Some of
these towers have been converted into
residences and, since the 1890s, the canal
has hosted the now biennial Venetian
Fete in August, with its procession of
floats and fireworks. The town is also the
terminus for the Romney, Hythe and
Dymchurch Railway, which has been
running its one-third full size steam and
diesel locomotives from Hythe to
Dungeness since 1927 and claims to be the
smallest miniature public railway in the
world. The beach and seafront promenade
are still as popular as ever.

The walk starts in the centre of Hythe

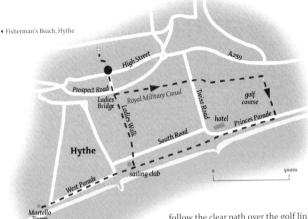

◀ Fisherman's Beach, Hythe

on the High Street by the columned façade of the town hall council offices. To start the walk it is well worth heading up Market Hill passage to the right of the council offices and doglegging left, then right to see the town's church. Retrace steps back down to the High Street. Opposite the bottom of Market Hill passage head along Marine Walk Street and over Prospect Road to reach Ladies Bridge and the Royal Military Canal. The route turns left in front of the bridge and heads along the raised bank beside the canal for 500m to Twiss Road. Cross over the road and continue along a pleasant track, which carries a bridleway and cyclepath, for another 500m between houses and the canal. At the crosspaths turn right over the canal bridge and, keeping an eye out for flying golf balls,

follow the clear path over the golf links up to Princes Parade and the sea.

Across the road turn right and you can now follow the esplanade on top of the sea wall for the next 1km, past the Hythe Imperial hotel and then seafront houses and apartments to the Hythe and Saltwood Sailing Club. From here, it's worth continuing and making the detour along West Parade by the sea for another 600m to Fisherman's Beach, where you can see the remaining working fishing boats and wooden fishing shacks on the shingle, beyond which are Hythe Ranges and a view along the sweep of the shore around to Dungeness.

From the sailing club, turn inland down the walkway to South Road, across which Ladies Walk will take you back past tennis courts and the cricket club to Ladies Bridge over the canal and the town centre beyond.

71

Hamstreet and Ruckinge

Distance 8km **Time** 2 hours
Terrain woods, fields and lanes
Map OS Explorer 125 **Access** bus to
Hamstreet from Ashford; trains from
Ashford to Ham Street Station, 300m
from the entrance to Ham Street Woods
along the waymarked Saxon Shore Way

**Wander through a nature reserve before
marching back along the Royal Military
Canal with views over Romney Marsh.**

Between Hamstreet and Ruckinge is a
stretch of the Royal Military Canal. The
canal runs for 45km from Seabrook to
near Hastings and, behind the series of
Martello towers on the coast, was a
second line of defence against the threat
of Napoleonic invasion in the early 1800s.
However, the expected invasion never
materialised, though the canal remained
garrisoned until 1842. After that a barge
service was established from Hythe to
Rye, but by the end of the 1870s the canal

had been largely abandoned. It is now
used to regulate water levels across
Romney Marsh and the footpath
alongside it has become a waymarked
long-distance trail.

The walk starts from the southern end
of Hamstreet by the playing field, where
there is a car park. Head along The Street
into the village and, at the Dukes Head,
turn right along Ruckinge Road for 150m,
and then left along Bourne Lane to the
entrance to Ham Street Woods National
Nature Reserve.

Here, follow the Saxon Shore Way and
Greensand Way, which take you into the
wood and then immediately to the left.
In 100m, around the right-hand bend, fork
right to stay on the Saxon Shore Way and
Greensand Way and follow the waymarks
through the middle of the woods for the
next 1km up to the gate at the top.
Continue ahead along the edge of the
wood up to a byway junction, where a left

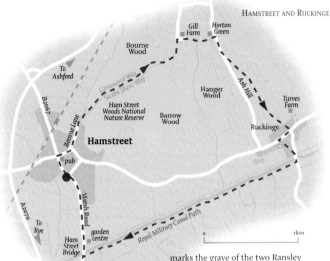

turn takes you in 150m to a track junction by Gill Farm. The two trails diverge here.

The route turns right with the Saxon Shore Way past the farm and then along the edges of three fields up to the road at Horton Green. You now leave the Saxon Shore Way and turn right down the road for 200m. As the road straightens out, look out for the stile in the hedge on the left into fields. Follow the waymarks over five fields, passing the backs of some houses and in the fourth field make for the fence ahead. Follow the fence into the large fifth field, whose left-hand edge leads you down to, and past, the Scouts and Guides hut into Ruckinge.

Turn right along Hamstreet Road to the Church of Saint Mary Magdalene. In the churchyard there is an unusual plank grave on iron supports, which legend says marks the grave of the two Ransley brothers. They were notorious local smugglers, hanged for highway robbery in 1800. The route continues to the left, across the churchyard to a gate into a field, where you can also see an unusual stone. This marks the spot of the end of a datum-line used in the attempt at the end of the 18th century to use trigonometrical measurements to calculate the exact distance between London and Paris. At the end of the field, turn right along the road over the canal and take the Royal Military Canal Path off right.

This gravel track takes you alongside the canal for the next 2.5km, with long views out over the marshland and past a brick pumping station to Ham Street Bridge. Here, leave the canal path and turn right past Hamstreet Garden Centre along the grass verge for 500m and then along the pavement back into Hamstreet.

◄ Looking past the datum stone to St Mary Magdalene's Church, Ruckinge

Stone in Oxney

Distance 6.5km **Time** 1 hour 45
Terrain lanes, fields and towpath
Map OS Explorer 125 **Access** bus to Stone
in Oxney from Tenterden, Appledore
and Rye (limited service)

**A secluded route around the Isle of
Oxney leads along what was once the
shoreline in Roman and Saxon times.**

Stone in Oxney, also known as Stone-
Cum-Ebony, is a secluded village
southeast of Tenterden on the eastern
edge of the higher ground still known as
the Isle of Oxney. On its southern side
Stone Cliff now rises abruptly from the
flat marshland and gives a commanding
view out over Romney Marsh. It is
perhaps difficult to believe that, before
the marsh was drained, the sea came right
up to the cliff. In the village, the 15th-
century Church of St Mary also contains a

surprise in the form of a Roman altar
stone and it is this that gives the place its
name. Originally carved on each of its four
sides with the figure of a bull, the stone's
carving is now only clear on one of its
faces. The bull was sacred to the Persian
god Mithras, whose worship was
particularly popular amongst Roman
military units. In Roman times, Oxney
was still an island and it may not be too
much of a stretch of the imagination to
wonder if this strategic higher ground
was used as a military post to keep watch
over the approaches to the Kent shoreline.

From the road junction in the centre of
the village, bear left along The Street in
the direction of Stone Church, past the
Memorial Hall and then the cottages and
houses of Stone Green, to where the lane
bends right up Church Hill. The route
now bears left up steps into fields and

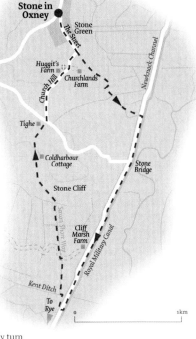

◂ The Memorial Hall in Stone in Oxney

follows the footpath across the first field and along the edge of the second down past rows of vines. At the far end you have to edge to the right a little to a gate to continue over three more fields to a footbridge across Newknock Channel by the Military Road.

Cross the road and head up onto the towpath of the Royal Military Canal, where a right turn takes you between the road and the canal on a rough grassy towpath for just over 1.5 km, past Stone Bridge and Cliff Marsh Farm to the Kent Ditch, which marks the county boundary with East Sussex. Keep on along the towpath for another 150m to a stile down onto the road.

Cross the road and join the route of the Saxon Shore Way back over Newknock Channel and immediately turn right to double back alongside the channel up to the Kent Ditch. The Saxon Shore Way now doglegs left, then right around the field up to a small ruined building by the track from Cliff Marsh Farm. Keep ahead up the track for 100m to the bend and then continue along the edge of two fields towards the prominent rise of Stone Cliff.

Cross the ditch by a footbridge and head half-left up a series of four more fields, in the third field passing to the left of the long-roofed Coldharbour Cottage, before bearing to the right along the edge of the fourth field down to the lane junction by Tighe house. From here it's a simple task of continuing ahead along Church Hill, over the rise and down past Huggit's Farm to the church, beyond which you keep on down through the bends and retrace steps back along The Street to the start.

Dungeness

Distance 5km **Time** 1 hour 45
Terrain paths over shingle and grass,
shingle banks on the beach
Map OS Explorer 125 **Access** bus from Rye
and Folkestone stops on Dungeness
Road by The Pilot Inn

**Make this unique journey around a
shingle headland just a pebble's-throw
from Dungeness Power Station.**

The headland of Dungeness sticks
prominently out into the English Channel
and walking on the shingle with the flat
expanse of Romney Marsh inland would
be a somewhat otherworldly experience,
even were it not for the looming presence
of a nuclear power station. The complex,
in fact, consists of two nuclear power
plants, an older Magnox reactor and the
other an advanced gas-cooled type. Since
being connected to the grid, in the 1960s
and 1980s respectively, both reactors have
now closed. Despite the closure, the
process of decommissioning means the
site will continue to be a feature for
decades to come, so too the need for a
fleet of lorries to continue to redeposit
tens of thousands of cubic metres of
shingle, which the sea relentlessly erodes,

in order to maintain the stability of the
headland and the safety of the site.

The walk starts from the Dungeness
station of the Romney, Hythe and
Dymchurch Railway, where there is a car
park. There is also a shop and restaurant.
Head out of the back of the car park, with
Dungeness Power Station on your left,
and follow the track parallel to the
railway to the start of a line of wooden
posts, where there is an information board
which commemorates two Polish pilots
from RAF 303 Squadron who were killed
during the Battle of Britain in 1941.

Bear left over the shingle and grass
towards the Old Coastguard Cottages,
which are surrounded by a large bank.
Go through the gap in the bank, where
birdwatchers can see the latest report in
the Dungeness Bird Observatory, located
in the last cottage on the left, and pass
along the backs of the row of cottages.
Just past the last cottage bear right back

through the bank and take the path which heads off to the right.

The footpath heads NNE across the shingle and grass towards the area of marshland trees and shrubs ahead, above which you can make out a number of chimneys in the distance, which serve as a handy marker. Pass through the line of wooden posts and across the line of a disused railway, whose wooden sleepers are still visible in places, to reach the low-growing trees and shrubs. The footpath now makes its way through the trees and shrubs for 400m, before heading over shingle and grass again towards the chimneys of Coastguard Cottages. At the cottages bear right up to the road.

There is now a choice of return routes. The quicker option is to turn right along the road through the gates of Dungeness Estate and follow the route of the England Coast Path back to the start. The longer option, and more satisfying one, crosses the road and passes along the backs of houses to the start of the shingle by The Pilot Inn, where there is a memorial of anchors, dedicated to those drowned in the Channel and to the lifeboat crews who come to the aid of ships in distress.

At this point, turn right across the shingle to the Lifeboat Station, where you can continue along the shingle bank further to the left, above the mean high water mark. The going can be tough where the shingle is loose, but the trick is perhaps to take it slowly. In the past local people used to adopt a simple, if now seldom seen, solution to the energy-sapping experience of walking on shingle by strapping boards on their feet. There are plenty of fishing boats, boatsheds and old workings to pause and look at along the way, in addition to simple beachcombing.

After 1.5km you round the headland by the new lighthouse, beyond which you can cut back inland on a boardwalk over the shingle. At the road, a left turn takes you past The Britannia Inn back towards the old lighthouse and the station car park.

◂ The new lighthouse at Dungeness

Canterbury is one of the best-known cities in Europe and is often mistaken for the county town. The narrow streets within its medieval walls heave with tourists at peak season, but the countryside around it has some fine villages, old mansions and woodlands. To the north, beyond the woods of The Blean and the dual carriageways of the busy A299, lie the seaside towns of Whitstable and Herne Bay. Further eastwards stretches the Wade Marsh, while inland are the low-lying fields of the

Stour Valley and the ancient traces of the now silted-up Wantsum Channel, which until medieval times stretched from Reculver to the old port of Sandwich and separated the Isle of Thanet from the Kent mainland by its tidal waters. In recent years the seaside towns of Margate, Broadstairs and Ramsgate have been undergoing something of a revival in popularity, reminiscent of their former heydays in Victorian times and the Sixties.

Canterbury, Margate and Sandwich

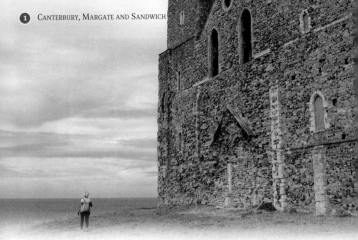

St Nicholas at Wade and Reculver

Distance 12.5km **Time** 3 hours
Terrain lanes, marsh fields and sea wall
Map OS Explorer 150 **Access** buses to
St Nicholas at Wade from Margate
and Canterbury

**A Roman fort and ruined church are the
focus of a longer approach over marshes
and a former tidal channel.**

Reculver Towers, the two towers of the
former monastic St Mary's Church, have
long been a landmark for seafarers, who
know them as the Two Sisters. Built partly
from stone taken from the Roman fort of
Regulbium, the towers still stand and, at
first sight from just north of the village of
St Nicholas at Wade, they seem much
further away than they are, in part
perhaps a trick of the light caused by the
open expanse of the intervening
marshland. There has been a church here
since Saxon times and legend has it that
this was where King Ethelbert converted
to Christianity.

Walk down The Street past the post
office to St Nicholas' Church, where there
is a memorial plaque to the Poet Laureate
Robert Bridges, and turn right down
Shuart Lane past houses to the footbridge
over the A299, beyond which Shuart Lane
continues for another 600m. At the end of
the lane bear left onto a footpath along a
track which takes you past Shuart House
and its farm buildings, heading
northwards over the fields of Wade Marsh
and across the railway line. Here, the path
bears half-right to reach the Northern Sea
Wall at Plumpudding Island.

You now turn left and follow the sea
wall westwards for the next 4km towards
the towers of St Mary's Church at
Reculver. The sea wall makes for

◀ The Reculver Towers of St Mary's Church

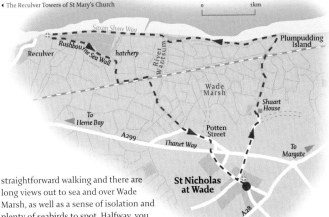

straightforward walking and there are long views out to sea and over Wade Marsh, as well as a sense of isolation and plenty of seabirds to spot. Halfway, you come alongside the River Wantsum, which brings you eventually to Reculver. It is hard to believe that at this point in Roman and medieval times you would have been out at sea as the river was a far larger tidal channel separating the Isle of Thanet from the rest of Kent, with the Roman fort of Regulbium set in a defensive position at the channel's northern end. There is plenty to explore among the ruins of the Roman fort and St Mary's Church; there are some helpful panels to interpret the history and layout.

The return route turns inland, 50m to the east of the wall of the Roman fort, onto a footpath which leads alongside a drainage ditch and then bends left at the pumping station. From here, you head past the shellfish hatchery on the raised bank of Rushbourne Sea Wall. After 1km,

where a side bank comes in on the left, drop down left off the bank of the sea wall and continue along the track at its base for 100m, before bending right up to the railway line.

The footpath turns left alongside the railway for 600m to a junction with a track, before turning right over the railway and the field beyond to a bridge across the River Wantsum. At the track junction on the far side turn right along the gravel track, which soon bends left, changes to a concrete surface and leads up to Potten Street Road. Bear left up the road for 500m to the houses at Potten Street and continue for another 150m to the road junction, where a right turn up over the A299 and along the pavement for 600m takes you back into St Nicholas at Wade.

Broadstairs to Margate

Distance 10km **Time** 2 hours 30 (one way)
Terrain seafront promenades and clifftop
paths **Map** OS Explorer 150 **Access** bus to
Broadstairs from Canterbury, Margate
and Sandwich; trains to Broadstairs and
Margate from Dover and Canterbury

**Enjoy an entertaining clifftop and beach
walk that leads between two of Kent's
most celebrated seaside towns.**

This linear walk follows the coast
between Broadstairs and Margate. The
walk starts at Viking Bay in Broadstairs, at
the bottom of the High Street, 600m from
Broadstairs Railway Station. This section
of the Kent coast has attracted many
writers and artists over the years.
Aficionados of Charles Dickens will
already know that, amongst the many
local associations, his crenellated clifftop
holiday home overlooks the northern end
of the bay and was renamed Bleak House
from the original Fort House. Margate has
a strong link with J M W Turner, the
'father of modern art', according to John
Ruskin. Turner spent time as a child in
the town and visited often during the
1820s. He famously declared that 'the
skies over Thanet are the loveliest in all
Europe'. In 2011 Turner Contemporary art
gallery opened in the town in a suitably
contemporary building and is passed at
the end of this route.

Head along the promenade towards the
northern end of Viking Bay and turn right
down narrow Harbour Street to the
lifeboat station and pier. The route heads
left along the sea wall below the cliffs of

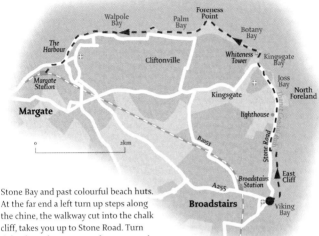

Stone Bay and past colourful beach huts. At the far end a left turn up steps along the chine, the walkway cut into the chalk cliff, takes you up to Stone Road. Turn right along the pavement for 700m up the hill to North Foreland Lighthouse. This was the last manned lighthouse on the mainland until its automation at the end of the 20th century and a lighthouse has stood here for over 500 years, warning ships of the treacherous Goodwin Sands, which lie just off the coast. Dickens thought that it 'stares grimly out to sea'.

Carry on past the lighthouse and down the pavement to Joss Bay, from where a cyclepath and footway heads up into Kingsgate. Keep on along the road past Kingsgate Castle and across the dip to the Captain Digby pub. Just beyond the pub turn right and follow the Viking Coastal Trail cycle and footpath which leads along the clifftops and turns left at Whiteness Tower, before heading past Botany Bay up to Foreness Point.

Here, you can switch to the lower path

by turning right down steps past the pumping station and left along the sea wall at the bottom of the cliffs, tide permitting. This path takes you westwards for the next 2.5km along Foreness Bay and then past Palm Bay, Walpole Bay with its tidal bathing pool and along to Margate's derelict Lido, the Winter Gardens and its lifeboat station.

Continue along to the pier, where you can see Antony Gormley's sea statue, *Another Time*, on the seashore near Turner Contemporary. Here, either head straight across Margate Sands or follow the sea wall and promenade past Margate's Old Town with its cafés and shops. The final stretch continues past the seafront amusement arcades to the far end of the Sands, where you will find the railway station a little off to the left.

◀ Viking Bay, Broadstairs

Sandwich and Sandwich Bay

Distance 6.5km **Time** 1 hour 45
Terrain paths over saltmarsh fields, golf
courses and beach **Map** OS Explorer 150
Access bus to Sandwich from Broadstairs,
Dover and Canterbury; train to Sandwich
from Dover and Margate

**A hands-in-pockets walk saunters over
saltmarshes to the sea from one of the
county's oldest ports.**

Strolling around the winding streets
and among the old buildings of Sandwich
it may come as something of a surprise
that the town was once one of the busiest
ports, not just in Kent but in England. Its
importance was centred on its proximity
to the Wantsum Channel, a wide tidal
channel which used to separate the Isle of
Thanet from the rest of Kent. Even after
the channel started silting up in the 16th
century the town's prosperity continued.
As a Cinque Port it also controlled access
for traffic along the River Stour, testament

to which is The Barbican toll bridge near
The Quay which, as late as the 1970s, was
still making a charge for crossing the river.
The route passes over the fields and
considerable expanse of marshland
between the town and the current
coastline of Sandwich Bay and shows
just how profound the change has been
to the landscape over the centuries.

From The Quay situated alongside
Sandwich Haven in Sandwich take the
tarmac path out of the back of the car
park, through a small park and past a play
area. Turn left across the footbridge over
the Vigo Sprong channel and follow the
Saxon Shore Way along the tarmac
pathway past a path junction with the
Stour Valley Walk and along Green Wall,
lined with an avenue of black poplar trees.
At the end of the trees the path kinks left
across an open field and then back right
to a footbridge across The New Cut
channel. Beyond the bridge the path

◂ In the dunes on Royal St George's Golf Course

becomes sandy and crosses a lane to reach the edge of Royal St George's Golf Course by its clubhouse and car park.

From here the Stour Valley Walk takes you past the clubhouse out across the golf course, where a series of white and yellow markers shows the way for the next 1km along the broad sandy path across the fairways and then through dunes to Princes Drive and Sandwich Bay. Across the road, the route turns left and you can walk up the sandy grass strip between the road and the beach or along the shingle on the seashore for 600m to the parking area at the edge of Sandwich and Pegwell Bay National Nature Reserve.

The return route heads along the footpath beside the entrance road to Princes Golf Club and then bears left with the Stour Valley Walk in front of the clubhouse along a gravel track for 300m, where the track bends right. Leave the track and keep ahead at the marker post on the Stour Valley Walk for the next 1km along a grassy path and over saltmarsh fields to a path junction by New Downs Farm. Here, a left turn with the Stour Valley Walk back over The New Cut channel takes you beside Sandwich Haven for just under 1km, along what was once the much wider Wantsum Channel, to the path junction with the Saxon Shore Way. Turn right to retrace steps over the Vigo Sprong back to The Quay in Sandwich.

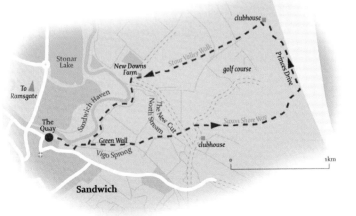

Stourmouth

Distance **7.5km** Time **2 hours**
Terrain **riverside paths and fields**
Map **OS Explorer 150** Access **bus from Canterbury stops along the route at the Rising Sun in East Stourmouth (limited service)**

Two rivers and two villages make for a varied walk over the flatlands of the Stourmouth Valley.

The shallow Stourmouth Valley now runs along what was once the Wantsum Channel. The Little Stour, which is followed during the first half of the walk and which meets the Great Stour a little further north at Pluck's Gutter, more or less marks the southern edge of the former Saxon shoreline before the channel separating the Isle of Thanet silted up after the medieval period. To the south, and along the route, lie the villages of West and East Stourmouth. The

settlements are connected by a public footpath, known locally as 'Church Walk'. West Stourmouth contains the parish church of All Saints. Its Saxon walls point to the fact that this is one of the oldest parish churches in England.

The walk starts from Grove Ferry Picnic Site car park beside the Great Stour, just off the A28 near the village of Upstreet. Head out of the far end of the parking area alongside the Great Stour on the route of the Saxon Shore Way, which takes you past the canoe hire centre, picnic tables and a grassy area on a meandering path for 600m to Grove Ferry Road. The Saxon Shore Way turns left past a house and along a track into fields, where it follows the edge of the first field over a drainage ditch and then doglegs to the right before heading left along the edge of a second field to a footbridge over the Little Stour.

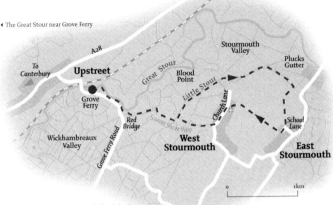

◄ The Great Stour near Grove Ferry

Across the bridge turn left with the Saxon Shore Way onto the riverside path, a little rough in places, which takes you past Stourmouth pumping station, then a patch of woodland and a bridge. Northwest of here, on a bend of the Great Stour, is Blood Point, whose name commemorates the 9th-century battle between King Alfred and the Danes, when he trapped their ships at this point in the Wantsum Channel. A little further on, a byway joins from the right and the river bends to the right to reach a second patch of woodland, fringed by some tall Lombardy poplars.

Here, leave the Saxon Shore Way and the riverside path and turn right onto the byway, no more than a path, along the edge of the woodland and then a field. Pass to the right of some agricultural buildings to a footpath junction and marker post. A right turn now takes you up the field past a Second World War pillbox. At the next footpath junction, near the top of the rise, fork left and pass over a track towards East Stourmouth, where the path heads around the edge of a field and past houses to reach School Lane. You can detour left down to the village centre and the Rising Sun pub.

The onward route keeps ahead along the upper part of School Lane and joins the Stour Valley Walk. At the last house, turn sharp right and follow this through an orchard, alongside a tall hedge and over a field towards All Saints Church and West Stourmouth, where you bear left through the churchyard past the church to Church Lane. Turn left along Church Lane for 300m through the village and at the left-hand bend follow the Stour Valley Walk off right alongside the hedge and between fields to the footbridge over the Little Stour, crossed on the outward route. From here you can retrace steps back to Grove Ferry Picnic Site.

The Blean and Clowes Wood

**Distance 6.5km Time 1 hour 45
Terrain lanes, woodland and fields
Map OS Explorer 150 Access bus to Blean
village from Canterbury and Whitstable**

**This country stroll through woods and
over fields is just a short distance from
bustling Canterbury.**

The Blean, situated to the north and
west of Canterbury, is one of the largest
ancient woodlands in England and has
been designated a Site of Special Scientific
Interest. It has been a working woodland
for more than a millennium and today it
is still a source of woodland products.
For centuries its alder, hazel and willow
woods supplied charcoal for the
gunpowder mills of Faversham, while
its oak trees were a source of building
materials and their bark was used by the
tannery industry in Canterbury. From the
18th century sweet chestnut was widely

planted and the 20th century saw the
introduction of fast-growing conifers.
Nowadays, the interest in renewable
resources has once more revived the
importance of the trees of The Blean.

The walk starts in the village of Blean at
the junction of the A290 with Tyler Hill
Road. Head along Tyler Hill Road for 100m
past the village stores and Blean Clock
Tower. Turn left along School Lane past
the village hall to the end, where the
route turns left up Bourne Lodge Close to
its junction with Chapel Lane. A right
turn down Chapel Lane now takes you
past houses and between fields to a path
junction by Amery Court.

Here, turn left onto the cyclepath, which
carries National Route 1 and is signed for
Clowes Wood. After 300m, where the
cyclepath bends left, fork right onto a
tree-lined footpath between fields to
reach the edge of Clowes Wood and a

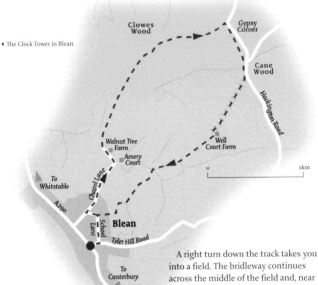

◀ The Clock Tower in Blean

crosspaths. Head over this along a narrow path for 200m through a younger plantation to a track junction. Continue ahead up the wide forestry track, which winds its way through mixed woodland for 1km to the car park at Gypsy Corner.

Turn right through the car park and, just before the exit, bear right onto a narrow path which weaves its way through the trees, parallel to the road off to the left. After 300m, it leads to a footbridge across a stream. Continue in the same direction for another 100m to reach a track and bridleway junction just down from the road.

A right turn down the track takes you into a field. The bridleway continues across the middle of the field and, near the top, doglegs left, then right to continue past Well Court Farm and along its drive. After 50m, where the drive bends left, keep ahead over two fields to a byway, beyond which you cross a small third field and head alongside orchards and a field of raspberry canes to the track carrying the National Route 1 cyclepath. A marker post points the way over the track and past more orchards to reach a stile into a field. Turn right along the field edge and carry on around the corner for 50m. Then turn right over a second stile and pass along the edge of a second small field to reach a walkway, which leads to School Lane. Here, turn left to retrace steps back to the start.

89

Chartham Hatch and Bigbury Camp

Distance 5km **Time** 1 hour 30
Terrain lanes, woodland and fields
Map OS Explorer 150 **Access** bus to
Chartham Hatch from Canterbury

Explore a delightful Kent orchard before marching in the footsteps of invading Roman forces under the leadership of Julius Caesar.

The walk starts from the top of Chartham Hatch village at the junction of Howfield Lane with Bigbury Road. Head along Bigbury Road past the village hall and houses. After 100m, follow the North Downs Way off to the left, in the direction of Canterbury and No Man's Orchard, along the right-hand edge of the recreation ground and a plantation down into woodland.

The broad path soon veers right and descends a holloway, bending right at the bottom of the slope to reach No Man's Orchard. The path keeps along the left edge of the orchard, where there are some benches and the public are welcome to wander among the trees. This is a traditional orchard and is one of only a few remaining out of the many that would have been found all over this part of Kent. The parish boundary runs through the centre of the orchard and the name is a traditional one for such a piece of land, which would not have been under the ownership of any one individual. Halfway along, there is an information panel showing the varieties planted.

At the far end of the orchard the North Downs Way heads through a gate into coppiced woodland and descends gently before bending right on an undulating path for the next 400m to reach a gate at a crosspaths below Bigbury Camp.

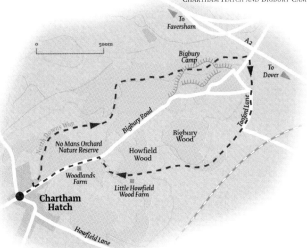

The camp is a major prehistoric earthwork and until recently was densely covered in trees, mainly larch, and also sweet chestnut, which was planted in the 18th and 19th centuries for the production of hop poles. Archaeological excavations have dated occupation of the site to 350BCE but it is also believed to have been stormed by the Roman forces of Julius Caesar on one of his exploratory expeditions in 55 or 54BCE.

The hillfort has been partially cleared of trees by Kent Wildlife Trust and you can detour to the right, off the North Downs Way, onto a footpath up the slope from where you can better appreciate the setting and layout of the camp. The route itself continues along the North Downs Way, which passes to the north of the main ramparts through the woodland to reach a second gate and a track. Here, the North Downs Way turns right for 200m to bring you up to Faulkners Lane.

Here, the North Downs Way heads off left over the A2 but the onward route crosses Faulkners Lane and heads over a stile along the left-hand edge of the field beyond to a junction with a bridleway and Tonford Lane. Bear left down the lane, where there are intermittent views out over orchards to the downs south of Canterbury, past a house and on for 150m down to the bend.

Here, leave the lane and turn right onto a bridleway which heads up into Bigbury Wood, before bending right over the rise, gently down across the dip and up alongside the fence of Little Howfield Wood Farm. At its entrance, keep on up the driveway for 200m to Bigbury Road. A left turn up the road for 500m takes you round the bend back to Chartham Hatch.

◀ No Man's Orchard, near Chartham Hatch

Bridge and Bourne Park

Distance 4km **Time** 1 hour
Terrain fields, parkland and lanes
Map OS Explorer 150 **Access** bus to Bridge
from Canterbury and Folkestone

**A short but near-idyllic walk weaves its
way across parkland to join a pair of
picturesque villages.**

This walk visits the two villages of
Bridge and Bishopsbourne, a short
distance southeast of Canterbury in the
Nailbourne Valley. Bridge is located on
what was the old Roman road of Watling
Street and still has a number of pubs and
shops. Bishopsbourne lies a little further
along the valley, separated by the
parkland of Bourne House, an impressive
Queen Anne mansion of 1701.

Bishopsbourne has an association with
the 16th-century Anglican theologian
Richard Hooker. In St Mary's Church there
are a number of memorials which record

his attempts at a time of great religious
conflict between Protestants and
Catholics to justify a 'middle way' of
tolerance, based on tradition and reason
rather than dogma and self-
righteousness. Also in the village is
Conrad Hall, named in commemoration
of the writer Joseph Conrad, who spent
the final five years of his life, from 1919
to 1924, living at Oswalds House.

From the centre of Bridge, walk down
the High Street to the bottom of Bridge
Hill. Just past St Peter's Church turn right
for 50m along Bourne Park Road, where
two footpaths head off left through a gate
into fields and parkland. The route now
follows the Elham Valley Way which forks
right over the shoulder of the field and
down to a gate into woodland. Bear left
down through the trees to the road and
then walk left along it for 100m past the
entrance to Bourne Park, where the Elham

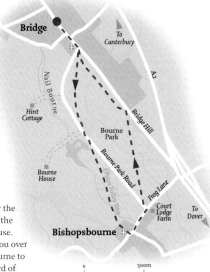

◄ St Mary's Church, Bishopsbourne

Valley Way heads off right over the fields and parkland in front of the red-brick façade of Bourne House. A couple of footbridges help you over a stream and then the Nail Bourne to reach a gate into the churchyard of St Mary's Church at Bishopsbourne, with Oswalds House to its left.

Inside the church, as well as the memorials to Richard Hooker, there is the stained-glass west window by Edward Burne-Jones and William Morris. At the junction beyond the church it's worth making a detour out and back along The Street through the village past pretty cottages and Conrad Hall to the Mermaid Inn.

The onward route turns left along Frog Lane, over the Nail Bourne again, and up to the junction with Bourne Park Road by a lodge house. On the right is Court Lodge Farm, which is home to the delightful

Tadpole Tearoom and a number of small businesses, including a bakery.

To continue, turn into Bourne Park Road and then take the fenced footpath on the right uphill across the upper part of Bourne Park, with good views back down over the park and the house. At the top a gate takes you into a wood, where you fork left just before Bridge Hill road and head back through a gate into the parkland. From here, head over the brow of the hill and back down to the gate onto Bourne Park Road, from where you can retrace your steps past St Peter's Church into Bridge.

Chilham and the Downs

Distance 9km **Time** 2 hours 30
Terrain lanes and fields with a steady
climb through woodland
Map OS Explorer 137 **Access** bus to
Chilham from Canterbury and Ashford;
train from Canterbury and Ashford to
Chilham Station, partway along the route
at Bagham

**From the well-known village of Chilham
cross the Stour Valley and climb the
wooded slopes on its southern side.**

Chilham has a picture-postcard
reputation and it is easy to see why when
stood in The Square at the top of the hill
overlooking the Stour Valley. On one side
are the gates to Chilham Castle and
opposite are The White Horse pub and
the entrance to St Mary's Church, which
contains some striking memorials,
including the Wildman Memorial and
Digges Memorial, and an ancient 1300-
year-old yew tree stump in its churchyard.
The other sides contain many timber-
framed buildings and it very much feels
as though not much has changed from
the medieval period. There is a car park
down the hill on the western edge of
the village.

From The Square head past the
entrance to St Mary's Church down
The Street, past The Woolpack Inn and
along the pavement to Bagham, from
where Chilham Station is accessible.
Follow the road round the right bend,
over the A28 and the level crossing
beyond, and along the lane to Chilham
Mill, originally a Victorian flour mill
which closed in the 1930s. Across the River
Stour turn left onto a footpath up
between the river and a house to a
crosspaths junction in woodland.

A left turn takes you down the edge
of a large field to Stile Farm, where the
path doglegs briefly right, then left to
continue in the same direction across two
more fields to Pickelden Lane. Keep
on past Pickelden Farmhouse along

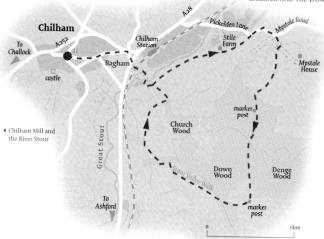

Chilham

To
Challock

A252

castle

A28

Chilham
Station

Pickelden Lane

Stile
Farm

Mystole Road

Bagham

◄ Chilham Mill and
the River Stour

Great Stour

Church
Wood

marker
post

Mystole
House

To
Ashford

Stour Valley Walk

Down
Wood

Denge
Wood

marker
post

0   1km

the lane, round the bends and up to a crossroads with Mystole Road. Follow the bridleway ahead up the lane for 100m and, just past Mystole Court, bear right to keep on the bridleway, which heads up a track into fields.

A little way into the field the bridleway forks right, off the track and down across a dip. Head up to the corner of the field and into the woodland to a junction of paths. Here, take the middle of three paths on the left to stay on the bridleway which leads gently uphill away from the edge of the wood. After 200m, at a track T-junction, turn right to climb steadily uphill for 750m. As you come out of the trees and the track bends to the right, fork left with the bridleway into fields. Pass along the left-hand field edge for 250m, beyond which the bridleway bears right up to a junction of paths at the top.

The onward route turns right and takes the footpath which leads across the field towards the wood and then down through the trees. After 250m you join the Stour Valley Walk, which keeps on downhill for another 400m and then forks right through a gate and on up some steps, before descending down a field to a strip of woodland. Here, dogleg left for 100m down the field beyond, then turn right through the trees, and head half-left across a third field to a stile down onto a byway.

Turn right up the byway over the rise and down around a sweeping right-hand bend for 250m to a footpath junction. The final part of the route turns left down a field, through trees and over a crosspaths to reach the River Stour and Chilham Mill once again, from where you can retrace the outward route back to the start.

Index